THE INSTITUTE OF POLITICAL PUBLICATIONS
WILLIAMS COLLEGE, WILLIAMSTOWN, MASS.

THE EVOLUTION OF INTERNATIONAL PUBLIC
LAW IN EUROPE SINCE GROTIUS

THE EVOLUTION OF
INTERNATIONAL PUBLIC LAW
IN EUROPE SINCE
GROTIUS

BY

WALTER SIMONS
FORMER CHIEF JUSTICE OF THE SUPREME
FEDERAL COURT OF GERMANY

NEW HAVEN
PUBLISHED FOR THE INSTITUTE OF POLITICS
BY THE YALE UNIVERSITY PRESS
LONDON · HUMPHREY MILFORD · OXFORD UNIVERSITY PRESS
MCMXXXI

CONTENTS

THE EVOLUTION OF
INTERNATIONAL PUBLIC LAW IN EUROPE
SINCE GROTIUS

I

THE STATE AND STATE SOVEREIGNTY

I HAVE been glad to accept President Garfield's kind invitation to give a series of lectures in this Institute of Politics, because the Institute seems to me to have envisaged the problems of politics in a truly scientific spirit. It not only invites that disinterestedness in all except the search for truth, which tends to eliminate the distortions of prejudice from our perspectives; but it conceives of politics in the broadest sense of the word. Its program deals not so much with the passing incidents of contemporary history as with the consideration of those permanent and deeper relations which, in the affairs of nations, tend to acquire the authority of law.

It has fallen to me in my own experience to have had an interest and to have taken some part in both these great fields of activity. As I note the varied program of this year's meeting, my mind goes back to historical events, some of which bear directly upon problems of current discussion. Mr. Garfield, in his introduction, alluded to some of them. I recall, for example, the exchange of notes between President Wilson and the last Imperial German Chancellor, Prince Max of Baden, whose legal adviser I was at that time, and the protest of the German delegation at Versailles, of which I was Commissioner-General

under Count von Brockdorff-Rantzau. More vivid
still are my memories of the difficulties and problems
of German foreign policy between the conference of
Spa and that of London, during which time I held
office as German Minister of Foreign Affairs. Then,
to turn to another page of the tragic history of these
vital years, I watched the inside history of the German Revolution as Director of the Chancellery of
Friedrich Ebert, to whom the German people owe a
great debt for his courage and statesmanship as first
President of the German Republic; and then, finally,
I watched the turning of a brighter page of German
history in the stabilization of the Republic through
the election of President von Hindenburg, who from
my hands—I was at that time Acting-President—received the office which he has since held and adminis-
tered so successfully in the interests of the German
people.

But it is not of these phases of political history
that I am to address you in the course of this and the
succeeding lectures. During the last seven years of
my official activity, I have returned to my old profession as a judge, a profession which occupied me
the greater part of my life; and since I was called
to the responsibilities of the office of Chief Justice
of the Supreme Federal Court of Germany I have
strictly refrained from meddling in politics. This
has remained my principle after retiring from office,
since I accepted the honorary professorship of international law, which I hold today. It is in this sphere
of jurisprudence, rather than practical politics, that
I have selected the subject of my lectures here.

In reality, however, international public law lies at
the base of all great political tendencies in the world's

history. For no great political movement has ever succeeded without the firm conviction of its leaders and followers that justice was fighting for them. It is these spiritual forces which I shall examine with you here, forces which brought with them first the anarchic conditions of the Law of Nations, ending in the World War, and then the attempts to organize humanity on a basis of justice instead of a basis of violence.

In doing this, it is my conviction that I shall be touching the most momentous political issues of our time. We are easily induced to think that the decisive factors of international policy today are of an economic character, and it is true, indeed, that the problems of international indebtedness, international trade depression, and international unemployment are of the utmost gravity. But to solve them statesmen must apply methods of international law. And even seemingly economic tendencies, such as international socialism, are dangerous only because they draw their strength and their radicalism from a widespread feeling of injustice in the distribution of wealth and power among human beings.

My attitude in the treatment of this subject of international public law must naturally be a European one, but I hope in spite of this fact to gain the interest of an American audience; for European and American international law are today less separable than ever, since the Great War has brought together both continents in a world cataclysm of blood and tears. We feel that since the Great War the world is in a period of transformation to an extent never before experienced. The differences of class and race override the frontiers of continents; a great experiment of communism is being carried out in an area representing one-fifth of the inhabited world, and is striving to spread out over the other four-fifths. Strife and restlessness are everywhere! But also new, heretofore unknown forces of union, of coöperation, of peace, are at work. For the first time a world organization has been realized—the League of Nations—the value of which, in spite of its lack of universality, cannot be overestimated. For the first time an international court has been established which really merits this name. In a completely new manner the Briand-Kellogg Pact by outlawing war has taken from the sovereign Powers a means of policy which was heretofore recognized under international law as the *Ultima Ratio Regum*, the last resort of sovereigns.

This, therefore, appears an appropriate time to trace history with a view to determining what means international law offers to the statesmen of today to master the new problems that have arisen. And it seems practical to start such a historical review with a man who, at the turning point of the sixteenth and seventeenth centuries, marked the transition from the Middle Ages to modern times, the Dutch statesman, Hugo Grotius, whose chief work was dedicated to the international relations between the states of Europe. A review of their development will show to what extent the vast transformation which the Law of Nations underwent during that period has been influenced by ideas emanating from the United States of America.

Taking the work of Hugo Grotius as the starting point of my retrospective survey, I am perfectly aware that today this great writer is not as highly

THE STATE AND STATE SOVEREIGNTY 5

esteemed by his living colleagues as when I began my studies in international law. Many learned lawyers, especially in the new world, attribute the honor of having initiated the scientific doctrine of international public law to the Spanish Law School of the sixteenth century. Last year, I heard on Columbus Day a very eloquent address of Dr. James Brown Scott, propounding the belief that Francisco de Vitoria, the learned Dominican monk and professor at the University of Salamanca, has a better claim to the title of the father of the Law of Nations. I do not deny his merits or his genius; he was the first to question the asserted right of his countrymen to wage war against the inoffensive Indians and to conquer their territories. But in my opinion his writings are far from having the thoroughness of research and the scientific method whereby Grotius has laid, for centuries to come, the foundation of international law. Vitoria, like his contemporaries and immediate successors, was yet too deeply imbued with medieval ideas and with the theological doctrine of his church, while with Hugo Grotius, the rebel and the Protestant, the Law of Nations begins to be secularized.

To be sure, Grotius was a theologian himself; in his eyes, the Bible was a textbook not only for religious purposes but also for lessons on international law. Confessing his reformed creed in a Catholic part of the Netherlands, he endured some years of incarceration. Grotius also was a humanist of marvelous learning, perusing the whole bulk of classical literature in search of evidence for his doctrine. And, last but not least, he was an active and practical statesman in the service of the Dutch Republic. More than once he was intrusted with important and difficult

negotiations for his Government, the States-General.
Returning from Sweden, where he had to arrange
some political business with Queen Christine, the
daughter of Gustavus Adolphus, Grotius died in 1645
on German soil, in the city of Rostock on the Baltic
Sea, then in possession of the Swedes. Three years
after his death, 1648, the frightful Thirty Years'
War was ended by the Peace of Westfalia. This peace
consolidated the independence of Grotius' country,
the Netherlands, formerly a part of the Holy Roman
Empire; it secured for the Protestant creed free expression in many parts of Europe; and it realized
many of the ideas which Grotius had brought forth
in his writings. So it came about that Grotius' fame
and influence overshadowed the glory of his Spanish
predecessor, to whom he was indebted for some important contributions to his work. Posterity saw in
him the beginner of a new era, the founder of a new
science, the father of the Law of Nations. Hence I
feel justified in reckoning from the publication of
his masterpiece in 1625 the period of European international law whose changes and modifications I
propose to describe.

The most striking difference between the medieval
system of European international law and the system sanctioned by the Treaty of Westfalia is to be
found in the notion of state sovereignty. Indeed, even
in Grotius' time neither the idea of the state nor the
idea of sovereignty was clearly and definitely conceived. The state in our modern conception is the
organization of a certain people settled on a limited
territory and ruled by a fixed constitution. The state
in medieval Europe (and in some parts of Europe
until the last century) meant a feudal group of the

people who by privilege and tradition had a right of their own against the ruler of the land. In the feudal system, the emperor or the king was not the direct chief of every subject in his land; he commanded the great vassals of the realm and was, for the execution of his plans, dependent on their obedience. When the German king wished to lead an expedition into Italy to get the imperial crown in Rome, he had to bid the vassals and free citizens of the realm to pay the Roman penny and start the military forces according to their feudal obligations; and when, in later times, the emperor was in need of help against the Turkish invasion, he was quite in the same position of dependence respecting the *Reichstände,* "the states of the Empire." And the princes and rulers of Europe, every one of them, had in those feudal times to reckon with his own states or *stände* or *états* if he was in need of money and armed forces for an extraordinary undertaking. The modern idea of a state began when the prince developed his personal wealth and finances by accumulating estates under his direct administration, by levying tolls and by indirect taxation of his people. By this means he was able to raise a standing army under his command independently of the good will of the "states."

In Grotius' time, this evolution had begun in many parts of Europe, but most of the princes were yet fettered and bound by the feudal authorities on which the superstructure of territorial rule was based. During the Thirty Years' War, General Wallenstein tried to free the emperor from these fetters by raising an army on his own account, directly sworn to the emperor, without feudal intermediates; he was murdered for his innovation. Not the emperor but the territorial princes had the best of Wallenstein's experiment.

During the last part of the seventeenth and the first part of the eighteenth centuries most of the territorial princes broke the power of their feudal states and formed the government of their lands and peoples in such a manner that the modern conception of state is applicable to their government, the conception of a paramount power to which every other will in the land must bow. Certainly this state was, viewed from the standard of today, very defective inasmuch as it was based on might and not on justice. In the administration of their territories the princes of that period knew neither legal bounds nor judicial control. When Louis XIV, the "Grand Monarch" of France, once issued an ordinance in contradiction to the law of the land, the President of the Parliament of Paris, Comte d'Ormesson, refused to inscribe it into the register of his magistracy and thereby to give the force of law to its articles; the King, furious, forced the Parliament by a so-called *lit de justice* to register the ordinance and not only dismissed the President from his office but banished this worthy nobleman forever from his Court—the greatest misfortune that could at that time befall a member of the French nobility. Another example: Once Frederick the Great, King of Prussia, was implored by the miller of Potsdam to interfere for his sake in a lawsuit; he got the impression that the High Court of his realm, the *Kammergericht,* had warped justice in favor of the miller's opponent, a nobleman, and he therefore canceled the sentence of the Court and threw the judges into prison. Historical research has shown that in this case the judges were right and the

King was wrong; nevertheless, by this arbitrary act he gained a mighty credit in the hearts of the Prussian people.

The father of Frederick the Great, Frederick William I, the most able administrator of his time, had smoothed his son's path by bending the recalcitrant leaders of the "states" of Prussia under his supreme will, declaring: "I'll establish the sovereignty of the Crown like a rock of bronze." And Louis XIV, when the states of France protested against some of his arbitrary measures, answered proudly: "l'état c'est moi." Under his weaker successor, the states of France regained much of their old right and influence, especially when the financial position of the Crown became untenable. At last the third state, the Commoners, won the preponderance over the first state, the clergy, and the second state, the nobility. At that time, a member of the clergy and a nobleman, the Abbé de Siéyès, issued that famous pamphlet on the *tiers état* with the motto: What is the third state today? Nothing! What ought it to be? All in all! This pamphlet was influenced by the Declaration of Independence of the American Colonies; it was the death knell of feudalism and absolutism and inaugurated the parliamentary system on the continent of Europe, the predominance of the *bourgeoisie,* whose ideal of a state was what we in Germany call the *Rechsstaat*—state governed by law. It was this ideal that Count Mirabeau, collaborator with the Abbé de Siéyès in the defense of the rights of the *tiers état,* expressed by the words "dans l'avenir, la justice sera le souverain du monde."

You will have remarked by what I have said that the development of the notion of state is intimately

connected with the evolution of the notion of sovereignty. There are two sides of this notion: an inward
side and an outward. Inwardly, sovereignty means
that power that may command every other power in
a given territory; outwardly, sovereignty means that
power that takes no command from any extraterritorial power. We have considered the inward side
of sovereignty developing from the embryo form of
feudalism to the matured form of a modern state;
let us now consider the outward side. Both are important for a perfect understanding of Grotius' position in the history of the European Law of Nations;
for in Grotius' view, international law is exclusively
the law regulating the relations between princes or
republics sovereign in their territories and independent of their neighbors. The third chapter of the first
book of his great work is mostly dedicated to an inquiry about the *suprema potestas,* the *summa im-
perii,* existing in the different forms of government;
Grotius makes this rather difficult inquiry with a
view of finding out which state has the right to wage
a public war and to conclude a solemn peace, in other
words, which state has the right of personality in international law. It is very curious to follow his de-
ductions taken from the Bible, the classic authors,
the usage of medieval times, and the examples of his
own period; he seems to be not yet quite conscious of
the great difference of the ages.

In the Middle Ages, public opinion in Europe knew
no bonds of international law existing between the
peoples of Christendom and the heathen nations.
There was private commerce between Christians and
heathens; there were holy wars to defend Christian

territories, to conquer the Holy Land, to subdue unruly heathen neighbors; but there was no system of common international rules, no force binding together the two worlds. When Frederick II of Hohenstaufen, a medieval emperor of modern ideas, ended his crusade to the Holy Land by a normal treaty with Sultan Saladin, the pope punished this outrage against the tradition of the church by excommunicating him.

Within the Christian world, public opinion during the Middle Ages did not acknowledge a plurality of sovereign independent states endowed with equal rights; it knew only two sovereign powers: the emperor, who brandished the secular sword over all the princes and powers of this world, and the pope, in whose hands the spiritual sword was laid by Christ himself. This doctrine prevailed until the time of the Church Reformation; it is explained in a most majestic form by the greatest poetical genius of the medieval age, by Dante in his *Purgatorio*. This famous Florentine poet and patriot does not claim sovereignty for his own mighty and flourishing city-state; he reserves the *suprema potestas* for the emperor. At the same time, he protests against the tendency of the contemporary popes to combine the spiritual sovereignty with a secular power. Even in France and England, the most self-reliant and independent nations of those centuries, the ruling dynasties began as fiefs of a higher liege lord. The French kings of the Capet, Valois, and Bourbon lines started as vassals before they grew strong enough to shake off the imperial yoke, to subjugate their French neighbor vassals and to give their lands in feud. William the Conqueror went to England as vassal of the pope, and King John afterward only confirmed this feudal relationship.

Martin Luther, protesting against the secular power of the pope as he protested against his spiritual sovereignty and denouncing both as anti-evangelical, admitted at first the political supremacy of the Emperor Charles V over the Christian world. But afterward he saw the necessity to intrust the cause of the Reformation to the territorial princes of Germany who adhered to his doctrine; so he was forced to sanction their open rebellion against the Emperor, justifying a felony by reasons of conscience and religion. This attitude of Luther was one of the most important causes of the decline of imperial power in Germany and Europe and of the development of territorial rights into real sovereignty. The vassals of the Empire became more and more independent princes. A long time before the Reformation, the mightier princes of the Empire, temporal or spiritual, by using their electoral faculty in nominating the head of the Holy Empire, had bargained many imperial rights for their votes; weak candidates of the imperial throne stripped the central power of one attribute after the other. Even the last chain that bound the states of the old *Reich* together, the appellate jurisdiction of the Imperial High Court or *Reichskammergericht,* was broken by many princes; the Emperor granted to his mightier vassals the *jus de non appellando,* the faculty of instituting a separate high court of justice before which every appeal in cases pending in their territory had to be brought for final decision. Think of a state of the Union gaining from president and Congress a definite exemption from the Federal jurisdiction, especially from the Supreme Court in Washington; a hundred years ago, this seemed not impossible—it would have meant the dismemberment of the United States, as the wresting of sovereign rights from the Emperor by the territorial princes, sanctioned by the Peace of Westfalia, caused the dismemberment of medieval Europe.

Some forty years before Grotius published his work on war and peace, the French author and statesman, Bodin, had issued an equally famous book under the title *De la République*. In the first book, chapters viii and x, he examines the conception of sovereignty and its true marks. It has been pointed out that his reasoning falls in with an Italian author of earlier times, Marsilius of Padua. This writer, an expositor of the Italian Renaissance, deducted from the attributes of the old Roman emperors the absolute sovereignty of their pretended successors, the emperors of the Holy Roman Reich of the German Nation. Bodin accepted the doctrine of sovereignty, but he denied that its attributes belonged to the emperor; he ridiculed even the dependence of the secular head of Christendom on his great vassals. He did claim those attributes of sovereignty for his king; and he was right, for the great rulers of France, from Louis XI to Louis XIV, including the Cardinals Richelieu and Mazarin, had contrived to suppress the resistance of the feudal *Fronde* and to build up a military and political power equal to that of the house of Hapsburg, the holder of the imperial scepter. Since King Philip Le Bel captured the pope, brought him for a long exile to Avignon, and extorted from him certain liberties for the Gallican church, the spiritual su-

premacy of the pope was no more of political account
for France; no one of her most Christian kings,
not even her ruling cardinals, hesitated to conclude
treaties of amity and alliance with heretics or Turks.

The same sort of sovereignty and independence
was acquired in Grotius' time by the kings and rulers
of England. The long wars of the red and the white
roses had decimated the British nobility and impaired
their power. The Tudors established an independent,
nearly an absolute, monarchy and refused to acknowledge any sort of imperial control or political supremacy. The spiritual supremacy of the pope over
England ended with the Reformation of Henry VIII
and the establishment of the Anglican church.

A hundred years before the time of Grotius, the
pope had enough political authority to divide the
lands of heathen peoples between the two colonizing
nations of that time, the Spaniards and the Portu-
guese. Under this title, both nations protested against
the later colonial enterprises of British, French, and
Dutch adventurers. But their title was challenged by
those younger nations, and with the decay of their
world power during the seventeenth and eighteenth
centuries they also were transformed into absolute
monarchies of the dominant European type.

Not only had the princes of Europe shaken off, in
Grotius' time, the supremacy of the Empire and the
pope; there were republican political bodies, once
forming part of the Empire, that likewise gained
liberty and independence. In the southern part of
Germany, where the Rhine has its fountainhead, the
peasants and herdsmen of Switzerland had freed
themselves from the tyrannical exactions of the dukes
of Austria and Burgundy; for nearly a hundred years

the Swiss foot proved superior to any feudal army and was respected as the most efficient military force throughout Europe. In the northwest of the Empire, at the mouth of the Rhine, the burghers of the Netherland provinces withstood their Hapsburg rulers and fought for their liberty and independence against the Spanish and other armies. After a period of long and bitter struggles, the States-General reached the position of a great European Power; for some time the Dutch surpassed in sea power not only the Spaniards but even the Britishers. To both these federal republics—the Swiss and the Dutch—the Peace Treaty of Westfalia confirmed liberty, sovereignty, and independence; they ceased definitely to be parts of the Empire. It is interesting to state the lasting importance of this fact: Switzerland and the Netherlands have lost their military power on land and on sea; surrounded by stronger states, they are reduced to a peaceful policy. But even by this policy of peace and neutrality they have contributed in not a small measure to the development of international public law in Europe. It is significant that the League of Nations has its seat in Switzerland and the permanent Court of International Justice in the Netherlands. In a period of absolute monarchies in Europe, those two republics were asylums of political liberty and self-government, and I think national liberty and international justice are in close connection.

We have seen that in the seventeenth and eighteenth centuries the removal of feudal institutions in most parts of Europe did not lead to political liberty of the peoples, but tightened the grip of the princes on their subjects. Every territorial monarch was emperor and pope in his land. By the Treaty of Westfalia the rule was confirmed that the religion of the people was determined by the creed of its ruler: *cujus regio ejus religio.* The Protestant princes pretended to be personally the highest spiritual authority, the *summus episcopus,* of their territorial church. This was the cause of the pope's condemning the Peace of Westfalia. No wonder that a statesman and philosopher like Thomas Hobbes, in his work *Leviathan,* described the sovereign state of this period of absolutism as an all-devouring monster. In Grotius' time, the word "sovereign" means a person, not an idea; and so to the sovereign prince is applied the ill-famed phrase of Roman antiquity: *princeps legibus solutus,* the prince is bound by no law. The absolute monarch is personally the fountain of law and justice in his land; in his name the judiciary give their sentence, but he may draw every case before his cabinet to be decided there for political reasons. On the other hand, the absolute prince and sovereign claims a perfect liberty in his dealings with other princes. This is not the meaning of Grotius; he vowed his work to the development of rules, half moral, half juridical, whereby a prince should be guided in the management of foreign affairs. Grotius tried to fix the notion of a just war; he was convinced of the binding force of that natural law that commands even princes to keep their word and to fulfil their treaty obligations. But the sovereigns of the period between the Peace of Westfalia and the French Revolution did not consider themselves rigidly bound by international or natural law and they were rather unscrupulous in interpreting and applying them. Confessedly or not, they proved to be disciples not of Grotius but of an older and yet more modern author, Machiavelli; whose *Principe* taught them even to break a solemn treaty, if the advantages that had induced them to conclude it ceased to exist. Indeed, the history of those times may justly be called a history of broken treaties. When Frederick the Great, as Crown Prince of Prussia, in disaccord with the King, his father, lived in a sort of exile, apart from political activity, he wrote his *Anti-Machiavel* to refute the doctrines of the reckless Florentine politician; but afterward, in his own kingly career, he acted more than once according to Machiavellian principles.

Sovereignty in those times was often conceived as being independence not only from imperial control and papal guidance, but also from international law. To be sure, there were many customs and traditions of international intercourse, the strict observance of which seemed necessary—for example, the privileges and immunities of ambassadors and envoys who represented their sovereigns. The rules concerning these things have not much changed since Grotius' times, although it has not been possible as yet to codify them; for there are always two tendencies contradicting each other: The sovereign who sends an ambassador wishes to secure for him as many privileges as possible, the sovereign who receives an ambassador does not wish to be hampered too much in his jurisdiction and administration by diplomatic immunities.

Last year the Institute of International Law in its New York conference again tried to codify this part of the Law of Nations; let us hope with more success than on former occasions.

The exaggerated idea of sovereignty prevailing in

the period of absolute monarchies was for the first time attacked on the Continent by Montesquieu and Rousseau. Montesquieu learned from British parliamentarism the advantages of a division of state powers; his doctrine of the reciprocal independence and interdependence of the legislative, judicial, and executive powers of the state was incompatible with absolutism and served as a guide for all believers in the excellence of a liberal government. Rousseau, by his theory of the social contract, struck at the very roots of absolutism, showing that even monarchs derived their supreme power from the will of the people, not from the grace of God alone. The American War of Independence worked for Europe like a test case proving the correctness of Rousseau's theory; indeed, the colonists of the new world by a social contract of the grandest scale, called the Convention, founded a state system, and chose a government. And this state system was molded upon the pattern of Montesquieu's theory.

The revolutionary forces of France tried to transmit the blessings of American freedom to the peoples of Europe; but they did it in a way not very different from tyranny. So the liberal movement that began with the declaration of civic and human rights —*déclaration des droits de l'homme et du citoyen* —ended with the imperialism of Napoleon. His wonderful career is marked by utter disregard of existing European sovereignties; he disposed of kingdoms and dukedoms as if playing a game. His fall brought a mighty reaction of legitimacy and with it came a remarkable attempt to construct for the continent of Europe a substitute for the Holy Roman Empire. The victorious continental adversaries of

Napoleon combined in the Holy Alliance and tried
to hold the nations of Europe, not yet perfectly cured
of the fever of revolution, under strict monarchical
control, while Great Britain stood apart and sub-
sidized the liberal factions of the continent. For both
parties the sovereignty of the European states was
not at all axiomatic; both claimed the right of intervention in any case where the Holy Alliance feared
the breakdown of a conservative government, or
Great Britain the tyrannical suppression of a liberal
or national movement. Now, intervention of a foreign
Power in the inner affairs of an independent state
is the worst affront that can be put upon sovereignty.
Consequently the states of Europe did not like the
tutelage either of the Holy Alliance or of Great
Britain. After an era of conferences between 1815
and 1830 (Vienna, Aix-la-Chapelle, Verona, etc.) and
an era of revolutions between 1830 and 1848, the idea
of the Holy Alliance vanished altogether; in its stead,
the statesmen of Europe looked for new forms of
international organization. They found it in the principles of European concert and European balance of
power.

These principles are of a political, not of a juridical, character. Nevertheless, they have sometimes
acted as if they were acknowledged rules of international law. When a prince of the Hohenzollern dynasty was elected king of Spain in 1870, France derived from this fact the right to protest against his
accession to the throne because it would disturb the
balance of power in Europe. On the other hand,
Prussia felt this protestation made in the face of old
King William as being an unjust intervention and an
affront upon her sovereignty. Bismarck's rebuff of

that intervention was answered by France with the declaration of war, of a war that changed the face of Europe.

During the last half of the nineteenth century, international relations were influenced increasingly by a new political principle—the principle of the inborn right of every national unit to have its own self-determined state—the right of national independence and sovereignty. In Grotius' time, the nationality of the subjects of a sovereign prince was of no account; most of the European rulers of that time had subjects of different racial and national character. But now the idea of the national compactness of a people began to predominate. The idea was launched by the ingenious Italian politician, Mancini, and it lay at the bottom of the crooked policy of Napoleon III. It was realized for the Italian nation by Cavour, for the German nation by Bismarck. But neither for the Italian nor for the German nation was the work finished; and in the eastern part of Europe there were empires comprising many peoples of different nationality under the government of a privileged nation. Everywhere, even in the kingdom of Great Britain and Ireland, the statesmen had to deal with difficult questions of Irredenta, of unredeemed national groups. These questions endangered the peace of Europe and threatened to disturb the balance of power.

To be more secure against such disturbances, Bismarck and other European statesmen resorted to a new system of short-term alliances. Ostensibly these alliances were destined for defensive purposes only; but by sharpening the contrasting interests and encouraging the weaker partners, they inevitably led to the final clash of the World War.

The Great War was for the sovereign states engaged in it—with the exception of the United States —a matter of life and death. No wonder that it showed in all these states, even in the Union, the inward side of sovereignty at its climax. The *droits de l'homme et du citoyen* were often neglected in an outrageous manner; the Leviathan of state, in its dire need, swallowed them one after another. But the outward side of sovereignty had often to bow before the exigencies of a war of alliance. These characteristics of the War cannot be considered as durable rules of international law; they are superseded by the peace treaties and the later practice of the Powers.

It is very remarkable that after the War both the theory and the practice of public law, national and international, have softened the rigid notion of sovereignty. The state, nearly omnipotent in the doctrine of writers like Hegel and Treitschke, is now on the point of being reduced to natural limits. In vain, members of the Viennese school of public law, especially Professor Kelsen, try to identify state and law; international practice, international treaties, and international jurisdiction agree with the more sensible doctrine that there are boundaries between state power and tyranny, state independence and international lawlessness. The peace treaties have acknowledged the rights of minorities as against their sovereign states; they have even instituted international courts to deal with individual claims of private persons against sovereign states—institutions unknown in Europe before the Great War, but reminding us of a similar jurisdiction of the American Federal courts. Above all, the peace treaties have tried once more to start an international organization not quite after the pattern of the Holy Roman Empire or the Holy Alliance, but designed for similar purposes. The League of Nations, to be sure, is just as unholy as the Holy Empire and the Holy Alliance, but it is, like these, a fortress of conservatism, and, to a certain degree, an assurance against excesses of sovereignty planned by its members.

We shall consider the questions of minorities, of international organization, and of international jurisdiction in later lectures. At the moment, it suffices to say that in the question of state sovereignty European international law is now returning to a standpoint more similar to that of the Middle Ages than to that of those centuries whose great teacher of international law was Hugo Grotius.

II

RIGHTS OF WAR

In my first lecture, I dwelt on the idea of state sovereignty as an example of the changes international public law had undergone in Europe since the time of Grotius; that is to say since European nations turned from medieval feudalism to a system of modern states, each claiming an equal right of independence from every other power without—and of sovereignty over every personal or associated power within the limits of its territory. As my hearers will remember, I pointed out the fact that Grotius developed the rules of the Law of Nations exclusively from the point of view of sovereign states—individuals or even communities of public importance but lacking in sovereign power are, in Grotius' opinion, not endowed with the right of personality in public international law. The test for this supreme right is, according to Grotius, the faculty to declare and wage war and to conclude peace.

His famous book that inaugurated the modern doctrine of international law or Law of Nations is entitled *De Iure belli ac pacis* or "The Law of War and Peace." You see, war comes first; the rôle of peace is generally limited to its function of ending war. In terms of today, the idea of peace is not a static one, a state or condition of good will and friendly commerce between nations, but a dynamic one, the conclusion of a treaty ending the condition or state of war. *Pax* meant originally a pact or treaty, and Grotius uses it mostly in this sense. The words *jus belli ac pacis* may be translated and interpreted in a double way: The laws of war and peace or the right of war and peace. In German terms of law philosophy (*Rechtsphilosophie*) the first interpretation aims at the objective laws or rules of peace and war binding all nations and sovereigns, the second interpretation aims at the subjective right of nations and sovereigns to go to war and to conclude a formal peace. The work of Grotius generally deals with both matters; but before it goes into detail it raises the question if men have a right to wage war at all and especially if Christians have such a right. After a very subtle examination, Grotius answers both questions in the affirmative. He further explains the difference between private war and public war. Starting from the principle that to wage a public war is only allowed him who has the *summa potestas* or *jurisdictio,* the right of sovereignty or of jurisdiction, Grotius nevertheless had to acknowledge that according to existing laws of his time there are cases where private war was not forbidden. Indeed, private war, in the Middle Ages, was under certain conditions a legal form of deciding a juridical contest; until very recent times, between free-born men the single combat as a sort of ordeal was deemed a natural thing, recognized by law and fought out under fixed rules. The duel between gentlemen, not quite extinct in Continental Europe, is the last remnant of this old form of applied justice. But in the time of Grotius, private war was waged in Europe on a much wider scale. The Thirty Years' War had seen a revival of the *Faustrecht* or right of private feud every medieval knight had claimed as his heritage. In spite of the truce of God preached by the church and the ban of the Empire outlawing the practice of the robber knights, private wars between the feudal grandees seemed inextinguishable. In some parts of Europe, wars between vassals had been sanctioned by solemn agreements; in others, there were even rules for armed resistance of vassals against their liege lord. So the Magna Charta of England gave to the barons of the realm the express faculty to use arms against the king if he should be found in grave default. Even wars between vassals of different sovereigns were, in the centuries before the Thirty Years' War, held justified as private wars when the interests of their feudal chiefs were not at stake. By the Peace of Westfalia, this difference between public and private wars was nearly abolished because the mightier vassals of the emperor gained full sovereignty, and the vassals of most European kingdoms began to submit their war-making capacities to the supreme power of their monarchs.

Nevertheless, some sort of private war subsisted until the time of Napoleon. According to the military system of the seventeenth and eighteenth centuries, the sovereign, it is true, was no longer dependent on his vassals for raising an army; but he often raised one in another and indirect way. He gave to a colonel the commission to organize a regiment under the latter's personal command; for the regiment so raised by recruiting officers (who often pressed the soldiers in a most treacherous and barbarous way), the sovereign gave the pay to the commander whose interest it was to be paid as high a sum as possible and to have his regiment clad, fed, and equipped as cheaply as possible. Besides these troops destined to serve their sovereign in a public war, there were troops raised by adventurers on their own account for private purposes or in the hope of being incidentally commissioned by a real sovereign for a public war. For the first alternative, I will only cite the extraordinary personality of the German Baron Theodor von Neuhof, who shortly before Napoleon's time played an operetta rôle as King Theodor of Corsica. His war against armed forces of the Republic of Genoa then claiming sovereign rights over the Corsican Island was on the verge between private and public warfare. As to the second form of noncommissioned warfare, I recall the fact that even Frederick the Great in his desperate struggle against three of the greatest military Powers of his time— Austria, Russia, and France—deigned to be helped by volunteering partisans who, without commission and without pay, ventured their luck in a private war against the enemies of the King, hoping to be indemnified after a common victory. Some of them, deceived in their hope, followed the counsels of Machiavelli and changed their party with a good conscience, as a not unusual thing under the rules of international public law. This sort of partisan or guerilla war is certainly not to be comprehended in Grotius' conception of a public and solemn war.

The Napoleonic Wars, by their grandeur, set an end to such campaigns. The expedition to Egypt may perhaps be considered as a big adventure of private war but, as a matter of fact, in fighting for his fame Napoleon fought, in Egypt as on other battlefields, a public war for France. Some partisans taking up arms against the conqueror without their sovereigns' commission, like the German officers Dornberg and

Schill, showed by the rapid breakdown of their enterprises that the time of such private wars had passed and the guerilla war the Spanish people waged against Napoleon was of quite another sort.

During the nineteenth century, the last resorts of similar enterprises in Europe were the Balkan provinces of Turkey. It is strange that after the Great War those old methods of private warfare seemed to revive. At least two expeditions of great international importance began as private wars, that is to say through persons not officially authorized by a sovereign power to use armed force for their political purposes. The first expedition is that of Gabriele d'Annunzio, attacking with his *Arditi* on his good ship *Puglia* the seaport of Fiume adjudicated by the principal Powers to Yugoslavia but claimed by d'Annunzio and the unanimous public opinion of Italy. He succeeded in this pursuit because the Government of his country defended by diplomatic weapons what he had conquered by force of arms, and the Government of Yugoslavia thought it advisable to put up at last with the loss of this important naval base on the Adriatic Sea.

The second expedition of a private character Europe experienced with some dismay after the Great War, was that of General Zeligowski. The city of Wilna was destined by the Great Powers to be the capital of Lithuania, but the Poles claimed it for their land. In former times, the Lithuanians and the Poles had a common dynasty; many families of the Polish nobility are of Lithuanian ancestry and many Poles reside in Lithuania. Therefore, without asking the Great Powers and without an ostensible authorization of his Government, General Zeligowski crossed

the Lithuanian frontier and occupied Wilna with
Polish volunteers. The Polish Government disclaimed
responsibility for this act of violence; but they bowed
to the fact and took the district of Wilna under their
administration. In vain the Lithuanian Government,
stripped of their capital, lodged complaint after complaint with the League of Nations; the League at one
time went so far as to send a small executive force
to the disputed area but until now the Poles have
remained in possession of it. For many years the
Polish-Lithuanian border was like a demarcation line
agreed between enemy forces during an armistice;
no friendly commerce was allowed, and on either side
of the new frontier troops were assembled ready to
fight. The dispute is still unsettled.

These examples show that even in modern times
private wars may be waged successfully; but nevertheless they are out of date because they are injurious to universal peace and disastrous to the
common confidence in international justice. Acts of
private violence upheld by state governments are
against the wording and the meaning of the Covenant of the League of Nations. It is an unhappy fact
that the League was not able in either case to settle
the conflicting national claims by mediation or arbitration. Fiume and Wilna remain, on this account,
very weak points in the European system of international public law.

There is an ancient and tragic counterpart in history of the Wilna and Fiume incident which is apt
to show how dangerous they are. When Rome contended with Carthage for supremacy in the western
part of the Mediterranean, both parties made a treaty
dividing the spheres of interest between them; but

the Carthaginian general, Hannibal, in opposition to that treaty thought it expedient for his country to extend its dominions in Spain. Therefore without a declaration of war on behalf of the Carthaginian Government and probably without their commission and authority, he attacked and took the strong Spanish city of Saguntum. Having been on terms of international friendship with this city and anticipating the ultimate aims of Hannibal, the Romans summoned the Government of Carthage to set Saguntum free and to punish their general as a pirate because he had acted on his own account. The Carthaginians answered: The question whether the general had waged against Saguntum a private or a public war was a question to be settled between themselves and the general, not between Carthage and Rome; with Rome they had only to debate the question whether the taking of Saguntum was a violation of the treaty. That was the origin of the Second Punic War, the most formidable war Rome fought in all her bellicose history, and the ultimate cause of Carthage's fall. Let us hope, and it seems certain of fulfilment, that neither the private taking of Fiume nor that of Wilna will have such terrible consequences.

Another form of private war that has played an interesting part in the development of international public law in Europe has been the practice of reprisals. Reprisals, in the Latin of Grotius, *repressaliae,* in French *représailles,* were forcible measures of self-redress used by anybody who thought that he could not otherwise get sufficient reparation for damage or injustice inflicted on him. Such self-redress was an acknowledged though turbulent form of securing justice in the Middle Ages; stronger sovereigns strove to make it legally dependent on their express authorization; but this claim was by no means generally recognized by the interested private parties. Even when this practice was in the era of absolutism made obsolete within the borders of one state, it remained a legal form of redress for injuries inflicted by the citizen of one state upon the citizen of another. Reprisals of this sort were not confined to a time of war between the states concerned but were especially employed in time of peace. It is a fixed medieval theory, on which I shall have to lay stress in a lecture on state responsibility, that all citizens are jointly responsible for their prince and for one another; consequently if an Englishman was in default against a Frenchman, and the Frenchman could not get his due through a summons, he took to reprisals against the first English goods coming his way. The international practice became very popular with the seafaring nations of Europe, so much so that French and English kings failed to stop it by ordinances and statutes; they were compelled to give it a legal form in conceding to their injured subjects so-called letters of marque under the seal of the sovereign. By these letters, the aggrieved party was authorized to make reprisals, that is to seize property of the countrymen of his debtor until he had recovered value equal to that which had been taken or withheld from him. Such private reprisals and the warlike expeditions of privateering captains based on letters of marque were apt to endanger all legitimate commerce between the nations concerned. Many captains contrived to get letters of marque from several princes in order to justify their privateering before the naval authorities of every state whose men-of-war they would probably meet. Against those abuses the different states of Europe provided by many treaties, in the time of Grotius and later. The Dutch statesmen were especially eager to secure the very vulnerable oversea trade of their people by treaty articles limiting or even forbidding the practice of issuing letters of marque. Louis XIV, by his *Ordonnance de la Marine* of 1681, established a procedure for grants of reprisal—the Admiralty was to examine and to assert the claim, half the amount of which was to be deposited as a security against abuses, and the property recovered under the letter of marque was to be adjudged in the same manner as war prizes. When the States-General, in 1710, concluded a treaty with the Sultan of Morocco, abolishing the right of reprisals altogether, Bynkershoek, the famous successor of Grotius as leading international lawyer of his time, recognized the progressive tendency of such treaties to oust reprisals. But he declared that, while a restriction of their use might be advisable, their total abolition was impossible because reprisals would forever remain the ultimate sanction for honest dealing between two private persons or two private associations who were not subject to the same prince and therefore had no common jurisdiction.

This opinion, however, did not reckon with the change of the European law relating to the international relations of sovereigns and subjects. In the time of Bynkershoek, princes began to realize that their sovereignty must be impaired by private wars waged by their subjects against subjects of other princes under the law of reprisals. As the fountain of law and the guardian of justice, each sovereign had the obligation and the privilege to take care of the redress for every injustice one of his subjects had endured from the subject of another sovereign; therefore the princes took reprisals into their own hands. I beg to cite two cases of a typical character, both famous not only because of the rulers who made use of reprisals but also because of the Powers whose subjects were concerned.

In the time of Cromwell's protectorate, the ship of an English merchant had been seized on the French coast by the naval authorities of the king of France. The merchant could get no redress for what he considered to be a violation of international law. He appealed to the Lord Protector. Cromwell furnished him with official letters to the leading minister of France, Cardinal Mazarin, bidding him at the same time to make another appeal should he not get satisfaction within a short time. The merchant was unable to get from Mazarin timely redress for the seizure of his ship. When he returned reporting the facts, Cromwell dispatched two ships of war with orders to bring in French ships and goods. The prizes were sold until a value was paid sufficient to indemnify the merchant for his losses.

Another example: During the European War in the year 1740 on behalf of the Austrian succession of Maria Theresa, Prussia was for a time a belligerent party, and for another time a neutral Power. During her neutrality, the British navy took Prussian ships and cargoes and British Prize Courts condemned them. The owners complained to Frederick the Great that they were being treated in a manner contrary to the Law of Nations. Frederick took the claims in his own hands and tried by diplomatic negotiations to get reparations from the British Government for the damage done to his subjects. He was unsuccessful. At last he appointed a committee presided over by the well-known Prussian lawyer, Cocceji, to report whether the British seizures and condemnations were justified, and if they found them unjustified, to name the amount of due compensation. The commission found that the British navy and the Prize Courts had acted in violation of the Law of Nations, that they had even neglected an Order in Council concerning contraband, and communicated by the British Government to the Prussian Minister in London. In their report, the committee stated as their opinion that the King would be justified in seizing the money Prussia owed to British subjects on account of a Silesian loan, and to make use of this money for the indemnity due to the injured Prussian merchants. The King acted on the report, and by doing so brought the British Government to a compromise.

In this way, private war of reprisals was merged, in the eighteenth century, in public measures short of war. On the other hand, private belligerent enterprise at sea did not cease in that century; it was of far longer duration. Although the kings of Europe from the times of the Tudors possessed state ships and important naval organizations, they did not feel it improper and against their claims of sovereignty to make use of their subjects' help on sea by giving them license to prey on enemy commerce on their own account. This practice became so common and at the same time so disastrous to every sort of commerce that many treaties bound the princes to demand from their privateers, before giving them the license, a large deposit of money as a guaranty against illegal treatment of merchantmen. They further required the captors to bring their prizes into port and to submit their capture to an admiralty court for condemnation. Nevertheless, abuses were frequent. To escape the formalities of the court and the dues every captor had to pay to his sovereign, many privateers sank the captured vessels and landed the crew on distant coasts in order to conceal the capture and to keep the goods. Against such hardships brought upon peaceful mariners, a treaty between Great Britain and France in 1677 provided certain humane measures—for example, privateering captains were forbidden to inflict cruel treatment upon a captured crew, that is, they were not to put them on the rack. The good credit Louis XIV gave to his privateers by such a treaty provision did not prevent him (in order to get information as to the enemy character of the cargo) from supplying even royal ships to private individuals for waging naval war on their own account. It is true, by Article 18 of his famous *Ordonnance de la Marine* he forbade to all privateers, on pain of death, the practice of sinking captured vessels and of exposing captured crews with a view to concealing the capture; but the interest of the privateers in getting booty undisturbed by law often proved stronger than kingly ordinances. The British privateering practice seems to have been no better than the French. In 1748, at the end of the War of the Austrian Succession, the British Minister at the Court of Frederick the Great wrote to the Foreign Office that undeniable outrages had been committed by British privateers upon the apprehension of an approaching peace and they had degenerated into mere pirates. The same outrages of British privateers are told by historians of the Seven Years' War and of the Napoleonic Wars. In spite of that, the British Minister, Lord Grenville, in a speech made in the House of Lords in November, 1801, said: "Although it may be true that occasional irregularities prevail, the country ought not to renounce such an important right as the right to license privateering."

The real disadvantage that governments sanctioning privateering had to trouble themselves about, seems to have been not so much the injury done to enemy and neutral trade as the frequent desertion from the naval to the privateering service. Life on a licensed ship was easier, more adventurous, and more promising of considerable gain even for the common sailor than the more disciplined and not less dangerous life on a man-of-war. So long as the proceeds of a capture virtually went to the captor and his crew, the predilection of captains and sailors for privateering was insurmountable.

In the nineteenth century, public opinion was aroused against this practice that seemed to be inconsistent with the humanity and civilization of the Victorian age. When the Crimean War threatened to break out, the Scandinavian states resolved to shut their ports altogether against foreign privateering ships or their prizes; but the British and French Governments published, in March, 1854, statements saying that it was not their intention to commission privateers. And when the Crimean War was closed by the Congress of Paris in 1856, all contracting parties, Great Britain, France, Russia, Prussia, Austria, Italy—then Sardinia—and Turkey, were unanimous in outlawing privateering by the famous article: *Privateering is and remains abolished.*

The contracting Powers invited all other Powers to adhere; but not all of them accepted. The answer that the United States gave to the invitation, the note of State Secretary Marcy, is of world-wide renown, a renown that has faded a little during the last seventy-four years. The Marcy note laid stress on the fact that the maintenance of a large professional navy was against the policy of the United States. It declared further that consequently the American Government would have to look to the merchant ships for the protection of the national commerce unless and until the seizure of private property at sea was universally abandoned; that, on principle, privateers were not more likely to disregard national rights than ships of the navy whose crews were often enough tempted by the prospects of winning prize money.

I do not know if the fitting out of the *Alabama* in an English port during the Civil War changed public opinion in the United States, because the *Alabama* was not, in a strict sense, a privateering ship. At any rate, the reason Marcy's note gave for declining the Paris invitation does not hold any longer in a time when naval parity with Great Britain is for the United States an object of compromise. In Europe, at least, all seafaring nations adhered to the Paris Treaty with the sole exception of Spain, who kept aloof until she lost the war of 1898 against the United States. Her adhesion dates from the year 1908.

During the last decades, the only question at stake in this regard, was if and to what extent it was consistent with the Declaration of Paris to transform merchantmen into warships in time of war. I will not dwell any longer on the niceties of this question and the negotiations that took place during the Second Hague Peace Conference of 1907 and the London Conference of 1908–9. The connection with privateering was broken when governments abandoned the practice of adjudging in each separate case of capture a reward in prize money for the crew of the capturing ship. I feel I have told you only too long and with too much detail the history of private warfare in Europe since Hugo Grotius. My excuse is a double one. First, that history is exceedingly characteristic of the development of the Law of Nations in Europe as a law binding states, not individuals; second, the history of privateering is, in my opinion, a good example of progress in the international law of war.

Privateering was a most romantic sport in the times of Sir Walter Raleigh and Francis Drake, but it was always very near piracy and lent itself to the worst abuses and outrages; in spite of that, as late as the beginning of the nineteenth century no great sea power held it possible to renounce this weapon. The Pact of Paris of 1856 did outlaw privateering in the same concise and solemn way as the Pact of Paris of 1928 outlawed war. Now, privateering after the first Pact of Paris vanished from the seas in a very short time, and I doubt if the United States in a future war would galvanize it into unhappy life again as a means of their national policy. May we not hope that the outlawry of war—a far more difficult and slow process—will have similar results? The Paris Declaration of 1856 is no guaranty against

Chinese pirates waging private naval war on the coasts and great streams of their widely disturbed country, and I think it would be a Utopian idea to assume that the Briand-Kellogg Pact will banish war from the earth. But in the same way as public opinion has abolished the legal piracy of privateering by attacking its claim for legality, so public opinion must abolish the legal murdering of men called war by attacking its legality under the Law of Nations.

We are very far from such a state of the public mind; I must frankly confess that I am even a little disappointed by the trend of feeling that seems to pervade many of the lectures and conferences I had the honor to attend here in Williamstown. When I came here I was certain that I would find in American optimism, American belief in the progress of mankind, in American idealism an antidote against the many doubts and cares created in my mind by the present international conditions of Europe. But my own doubts and cares are, until now, rather aggravated by what I have heard.

Take, for example, the matter of disarmament. The history of armament in Europe is, since the Middle Ages, a very complicated one. The feudal armies were superseded rather by the prowess of a people in arms fighting for their liberty—the Swiss —than by the invention of gunpowder. When the Swiss made a bargain of their belligerent force soldiering in the wars of foreign princes, their force was broken in the sixteenth century by the German *lansguenets* in the great battle of Pavia, the Swiss fighting for the king of France, the Germans for their emperor. During the next two centuries, absolute princes created standing armies of hired troops, mostly recruited or pressed without great regard as to their nationality, but with regard to the finances of the sovereign. France was then the great military preceptor of Europe; since that time, French words for military affairs have remained in use throughout the world. The American War of Independence showed afresh what success a people fighting for its liberty may obtain even with untrained troops. The American example was followed by the people of France fighting for their republic against the monarchical coalitions. M. Mantoux, the other day, gave us very interesting data about the conscript armies of France levied during the Republican and Napoleonic Wars. From that time onward, the competition in armaments did not stop in Europe; Prussia first, then the other continental nations followed the new French example. There is only one opinion about the danger of such a competition. The government of a nation in arms is bound to give it the best and strongest armament possible, and every new invention in military technique increases the financial burdens and the political dangers of the competing states.

I must abstain from recalling the attempts of the European Powers before and after the Great War to come to an agreed limitation of armaments; this chapter has been dealt with by more competent speakers. I only wish to point out that, from a German point of view, disarmament in Europe is not any longer a question of pure international policy and opportunity but that it has become a question of international law and international obligation. By the Covenant of the League of Nations, the members of the League, in Article 8, have solemnly declared that the maintenance of peace requires the reduction of armaments to the minimum consistent with national security, and with the execution of the international obligations which a common action would impose. The Article provides a procedure to reach a common plan of reduction, after whose adoption by the League none of its members may raise its armament above the agreed level without the consent of the Council. The procedure has now worked ten years without any success comparable with the results of the Washington Conference of 1922 or the last London Conference. This may be annoying to such members of the League as hoped to gain financial relief and greater political security by a general reduction of armaments; but after all no European state can complain that such reduction has not yet been effected so long and so far as this state keeps its liberty of action to raise its own armament to that level it thinks fit and necessary for its individual purposes. On the other hand, this situation is unbearable for the former Central Powers forced by the peace treaties of 1919 to reduce their armaments in the numbers and equipment of troops and ships to a degree not negotiated under Article 8, but dictated by the winners of the War—a situation that makes the Central Powers nearly helpless in case of an attack directed against them by any of their neighbors. The treaties, especially the preamble to the military, naval, and air clauses, declare that the forced disarmament of the Central Powers is the condition and the beginning of general disarmament; it is a sort of earnest; therefore, the Central Powers, by a general rule of international law, have a good consideration in claiming a more rapid and a more effective reduction of the armaments of League members than has been attempted until now.

The current word for this problem is "disarmament"; but it is not the right word. Total disarmament is in the view of a practical statesman quite out of the question; for the essence of state is might and to keep the power of subduing evildoers within, and of defending its territory against attacks from without, the state undoubtedly must retain armament. This was pointed out very clearly this morning in the General Conference by Admiral Hepburn and M. Mantoux. Article 8 of the Covenant has in view not disarmament but reduction of armaments to the necessary minimum, adding to the conditions of inner and outward security the new item of responsibility under Article 16 of the Covenant in case of League sanctions. Now what has been tried until now by the League Commissions and by the Conferences of Washington and London is by no means such a reduction, but only a limitation of armaments, sometimes a limitation of existing armaments, sometimes a limitation of future armaments. There are even Powers that have claimed, under the head of limitation, an armament stronger than their situation at that time allowed them to build up. Now, this sort of limitation of armaments may save money but it never will save peace; moreover, it is by no means a fulfilment of the obligations which the signatory Powers of the peace treaties solemnly incurred when they disarmed the Central Powers. They always plead security when they oppose effective reduction; but they forget that Germany, Austria, Hungary, and Bulgaria have now, a dozen years after the War, the same claim to security which their neighbors have.

Unilateral disarmament is no durable system between members of the same League, who ought to be equally independent and self-respecting nations; therefore, it seems to me that to avoid changes of an arbitrary and dangerous character, statesmen and experts of the League should make every effort to come to an early solution of this problem. I think I know its difficulties because I was ordered to find them out with other experts in preparing the Second Hague Peace Conference. In both conferences, the German delegates have explained the difficulties clearly enough but I know also that where there's a will there's a way.

In my opinion the problem of humanizing war is even more difficult than the problem of reduction of armaments. Its history is full of changes and of reactions after progress. Every new military device has been received by protestations because of its barbarity and lack of chivalry, and nevertheless every device has been made use of to its uttermost possibilities. Grotius in his work on war and peace calls the restrictions put into warfare by the humanizing tendency of the Law of Nations *temperamenta,* rules tempering or softening the hard law of war: rules not to kill all enemies, not to devastate all enemy towns and properties, not to take more enemy goods than is necessary for the purposes of the war, and so on. These rules Grotius published when the Thirty Years' War raged through central Europe; how well they were followed by the armies is a fearful and often-told tale. It was mostly a question of discipline. When, some years before the war, the Duke of Alba made his famous march from Genoa to Antwerp, the Spaniards under his command behaved like true *caballeros,* doing no harm and paying for what they wanted. When Gustavus Adolphus began his German campaign, the Swedish soldiers of this pious King showed an exemplary discipline; Wallenstein's troops were known to have been restrained from arbitrary cruelties, plunderings, and devastations by the iron will of their commander. On the other hand, General Tilly gave to his troops the old-fashioned right of three days' plundering in every defended city he could take; the city of Magdeburg, one of the richest of the Empire, was robbed, burnt down, and more than twenty thousand of her inhabitants were slain by the infuriated soldiery; after the siege of New Brandenburg, Tilly ordered the whole Swedish garrison, three thousand men, to be slaughtered as a punishment for their long and valiant defense of the town. In the later years of the war, the discipline of all troops gave way, and Spaniards and Swedes alike left in Germany the reputation of having behaved like very fiends. Humane treatment shown the captives and the civil population in enemy countries has always alternated with acts of revenge and barbarism; in this respect, there was no difference between the standing armies of absolute monarchs and the untrained troops of a people in arms. All prolonged wars and all wars against guerilla troops have ended in a lack of humanity. In the correspondence of the Duke of Wellington, we find many marks of the difficulty this great man had to keep his troops disciplined. After the victory of Vitoria, he wrote: "We started with the army in the highest order and up to the day of battle nothing could be better, but that event has as usual totally annihilated all order and discipline." I shall not go further into details and shall make only two comments about humanity in the Great War: First, that the troops of the Allied and Associated Powers had no occasion to prove their discipline through four years' fighting in enemy territory; second, that the combination of the blockade and the contraband system operated against Germany during the War and eight months after the armistice cannot be described as a means of humanizing war even if it was meant as a means to shorten it.

The outstanding problems regarding modern humanization of warfare are now the problems of chemical and aerial warfare, as in the nineteenth century they concerned the treatment of wounded soldiers and prisoners of war. In this respect, the Crimean War of 1854–55 was distinguished by the active charity of Florence Nightingale, the Italian War of 1859 by the similar spirit of Henri Dunant. The Red Cross founded by Dunant has now undertaken to secure the civil populations of belligerent states against the horrors of chemical and aerial warfare. I am sorry to disagree with such an expert as Edward P. Warner in the estimate of these horrors.

The International Red Cross has asked my opinion about the possibility of procuring a greater security against aerial bombardments by rules of international law. I have studied the discussions that took place during the two conferences of the Experts Committee of the Red Cross in Brussels and in Rome these last years, and I am convinced that neither technical nor legal measures can give real security, and that the consequences of aerial warfare for the civil population of great cities must be most horrible, especially in the case of nations who have no military aircraft ready for the defense of industrial centers against sudden attacks of bombarding squadrons. So I come to the conclusion that the endeavors of the Red Cross are doomed to futility, because no nation reckoning with a future war will renounce the most effective weapon that human intelligence and inventiveness has ever procured for military purposes, and that the only means to overcome the danger of aerial war is to overcome war itself.

But is this possible? Must we not at least retain war as a common sanction of an organized society of states against a criminal state which has deliberately neglected its international obligations or ruthlessly broken the peace of the world? This question leads us back to the doctrine of Grotius of a just war. Grotius by this doctrine paid his tribute to the old school of theologians and lawyers who took pains to reconcile the necessities of politics with the teaching of Christ and the doctrine of the Christian church. Grotius' attempts to define the causes of a just war are very ingenious and backed by an immense learning; but they were inevitably wrecked on the reef of sovereignty. Grotius himself and his country, the States-General of the Netherlands, had shaken off the supremacy of the pope and the emperor, so the conscience of the sovereign prince was left to decide if the war waged was just. Therefore, the disciples of Grotius abandoned the theory of *justum bellum*, of the just war; especially Emeric Vatel, a Swiss who wrote in French, and was the most influential author on international law of his time. He claimed for each sovereign prince the right to decide for himself if he was justified in declaring war. In this way, European civilization returned to the doctrine of Greek and Roman antiquity, teaching that war was a legal means for every aim of national policy such as glory, wealth, enlargement of territory or revenge, and prevention of a possible attack.

The League of Nations has changed this attitude of modern states. The Covenant is framed with a view to eliminate war between members of the League as far as possible; they are duly allowed to wage war if they have tried all peaceful means that the League has in store for them and if these means have failed. On the other hand, the Covenant provides the application of common force against a member that disobeys a unanimous mediation proposal of the Council or the Assembly of the League, that disobeys a sentence of an international court of justice or arbitration, or that breaks the general peace by a war of aggression. So we find anew the distinction of Grotius between a just war—that is the war of sanction or of execution, the war of the League—and the unjust war, that is the war of aggression or the war of defense against the League. Furthermore, we find anew the distinction of Grotius between a public war and a private war; the public war—that is the general war decreed by the League; the private war, that is the war waged justly or unjustly by one member of the League against another member.

It is a problem well worth the intense study of international lawyers to determine how far the rules of international law respecting war are applicable to the wars of the League sanctioning international sentences or punishing a peace-breaking state. Another problem much more in the searchlight of international law is the adaptation of the Covenant to the

Briand-Kellogg Pact. The Pact forbids private war
as a means of national policy, even a war which the
Covenant allows, but the Paris Pact allows a League
war as a means of international policy. The gap in
the Pact of Paris is this: That a state, member of
the League, which is injured by another member and
cannot find redress by the peaceful means of the
Covenant, gets no help by the Pact in the place of
the forbidden private war; so it seems to me that the
League, under the Paris Pact, is more than ever in
need of the Geneva Protocol of 1924 destined to fill
up the corresponding gap in the Covenant.

On the other hand, I doubt very much if the practice of sanctions and enforcements will prove a bless-
ing for the League. History tells us that every society of nations breaks asunder when it tries to subdue one of its members by armed force. The old
Greek League of Nations, called the *Amphiktyones,*
was destroyed by the Holy Wars, the wars of sanction it waged against one of its members being
in default, and especially because it was compelled
to leave the burden of the war to the strongest
Power, Macedonia, who thereby gained hegemony
and brought the liberty of Greece to an end. I verily
believe a better and surer way, even if it is a longer
and more difficult one, is the education of the world's
public opinion, an education in order to strengthen
the sense of fidelity to treaty obligations, of good
will and mutual understanding, abhorrence of war
and respect for the authority of international courts.
The German people has, in the Weimar Constitution,
ratified the following articles:

Rules of international law generally acknowledged
are binding parts of German Federal law.

Education in all German schools must be directed in the spirit of national tradition and international conciliation.

I am sure these are principles of general applicability, and if generally applied, they would go farther in outlawing war and securing peace than any military sanctions.

NOTE. For some of the facts referred to in this and other lectures, I am indebted to the work of the late Sir Geoffrey Butler and Mr. Simon Macoby on *The Development of International Law* (1928).

III

RIGHTS OF NEUTRALITY

NEUTRALITY is a corollary to war. Consequently, when the conception of war has changed in Europe since Grotius, as I have tried to prove in my second lecture, the conception of neutrality must likewise have changed. That this has really been the case, you can see by a very simple outward sign. If you compare with the standard work of Grotius any modern handbook on the Law of Nations, you will find that in the modern book the doctrine of neutrality takes a big place; indeed, only to comment upon the two Hague Conventions of 1907 regarding neutrality on land and sea, requires a great many pages. In Grotius' work, on the other hand, neutrality is discussed in one small chapter of the last book, one chapter out of fifty-six of the whole work; in my copy of an old Amsterdam edition of 1651, published a few years after the author's death with his latest annotations, the chapter on neutrality takes four pages out of 576. Even the word "neutrality" is not used by our author; he paraphrases the condition of neutrality by the words *de his qui in bello medii sunt*—"on those who are between in the war." It seems therefore not surprising that the majority of modern writers of the Law of Nations will not acknowledge an early origin of the Law of Neutrality; they assert that it is of quite recent date. In my opinion this customary assertion is not founded on facts. The expression used by Grotius to indicate neutrals, *medii in bello,* is

classic Latin; the Romans knew neutrality quite well
and had their theories concerning it. They knew that
when two parties were fighting a third party may
have an interest in keeping aloof from the combat.
It is an old Roman truism: *duobus litigantibus ter-
tius gaudet*—"when two are fighting the third has
the best of it." Later on, in the time of Rome's growing imperialism, they ceased to make much of neutrality; if they had to fight a foe, they demanded
other nations to send auxiliaries, or else they also
fought these nations. It is an official declaration made
by the Senate of Rome to the government of a nation that preferred to stay neutral: *Romanos aut
amicos aut hostes habere oportet; media via non est*
—"you must be either the allies or the enemies of
Rome; there is no neutrality." Imperialism always
was an antagonist of neutrality, while in a society
of independent sovereign states, especially when
there is some balance of power between them, neutrality is deemed of greatest value. That was the
case in ancient Greece; consequently we find in Greek
history that certain rules of neutrality were observed
which remind us of corresponding articles of the
Hague Neutrality Conventions. For example, when
Athens, in the course of their thirty years' war
against Sparta, began their ill-omened expedition to
Sicily, they fitted out a mighty fleet of warships and
transports and sent it to the nearest coast of southern Italy, which was then called Greater Greece because of its many Greek colonies. The expedition was
directed against Syracuse, a Doric colony and an
ally of Doric Sparta; the colonies of southern Italy,
however, were mostly of Ionian origin, and were
partly founded by Athens. So the Athenians reck-

oned on the help of those Ionian cities; but the Ionians, in doubt about the success of the expedition, because the Athenians had begun their campaign by banishing their ablest general, admiral, and statesman, Alkibiades, declared themselves neutral. When the leader of the expedition demanded entrance into their ports in order to use them as naval and strategic bases against Sicily, they refused and even declined to provide the fleet with stores and supplies for the campaign, and they only allowed the ships that quantity of water and food supply necessary to reach the next port. This attitude of neutrality taken by the deemed allies was one of the causes of the failure of the great expedition to Sicily. There are two great wars of purely Greek history; Alexander was not Greek by race. Of these two wars one created the international prestige of Greece while the other destroyed it. Both sprang from violated neutrality obligations. The Persian War began, when Athens, at peace with Persia, gave hostile assistance to the Ionian city of Mitylene, then at war with Persia, and sent ships to her rescue. The Peloponnesian War began when Athens took the same unneutral measure in the war between Corinth and the Ionian island state of Kerkyra, that is now Corfu.

I recall these facts to show that a man of Grotius' learning would have had ample opportunity to go deeper into the question of neutrality than he actually did; but as I have pointed out in my former lecture, he was not quite free from medieval reminiscences, and indeed, during the Middle Ages, neutrality was not a question of political importance or an object of juridical research. Minor wars, especially private wars of smaller vassals, were localized

by the nature of the contest or of the theater of war
(not by a declaration of neutrality issued by neighbor states), while wars of a general character, like
the campaigns of the emperors in Italy or the Crusades, left no legal place for neutrality. When Frederick Barbarossa began his campaign in northern
Italy in order to secure for himself the crown of the
Holy Roman Empire, he claimed the assistance of
all his vassals. But one of them, Henry the Lion,
Duke of Saxony, head of the Welf dynasty, whose
last offspring is now son-in-law of Emperor William
II, refused assistance, and thereby caused Frederick's grave defeat in the battle of Legnano lost
against the City League of Lombardy. Henry's attitude then was not neutrality, but felony.

On the other hand, many wars were then going
on in the world of which European Powers had no
knowledge at all. When the Aztecs came to Mexico,
overthrowing the Kingdom of the Toltecs in the
fourteenth century, neither the Republic of Genoa
nor the king of Castilia had anything to do with this
war, for the time had not yet come when the citizen
of Genoa and Admiral of the Crown of Castilia,
Christoforo Colombo or Cristobal Colon, had found
the way to the new world. But it would be impossible
to say that Genoa or Castilia was neutral in that war
between Aztecs and Toltecs; to be neutral in a war
a Power must know about it. But there is another
supposition: To be neutral, the Power in question
must not only know about the war, but also be able
to take part in it. The German Government may have
been informed by the newspapers of the warlike action that the tribe of the Afridis has just now undertaken at the eastern frontier of British India; but it

would be ridiculous to say that Germany with regard to this war is neutral. Neutrality is not only a fact but a resolution; the nearer the territory of a state not primarily involved in the struggle lies to the seat of war, the greater is the danger of its being entangled, the greater also the need of a firm resolution to remain neutral.

One of the first examples of such a resolution in Grotius' time is the declaration of neutrality which the Swiss sent to the emperor in 1638 when he asked their help in the Thirty Years' War. In this declaration, the word neutrality is used for the first time in a political document. The importance, however, lies not in the nomenclature but in the fact that it is the foundation of the international legal status of Switzerland as an independent and constitutionally neutral nation. Swiss *independence* was generally recognized by the Treaty of Westfalia, ten years after the declaration; Swiss *neutrality*, which was also often stipulated by separate treaties with many European Powers, did not find a general acknowledgment until the Peace of Vienna in 1815, 177 years later. As a matter of fact, the political principle of neutrality did not prevent the Swiss Confederacy from allowing some belligerent prince to recruit in Switzerland thousands of Swiss soldiers, sometimes by a unilateral treaty, sometimes in competition with his enemy. Even after the Peace of Vienna, when Swiss neutrality was an acknowledged part of the international public law of Europe, Switzerland made treaties with European kingdoms with the purpose of providing them with troops for the wars they had to wage. In 1816, the Swiss allowed the king of France to recruit two guard and two line regiments;

in 1824 they offered facilities to the king of Naples for the enlistment of four regiments. The exportation of soldiers had proved so good a bargain for the Swiss cantons that they were reluctant to renounce the practice. Moreover, they had on their side the authority of Emeric Vatel, the great international lawyer of the eighteenth century. Vatel explained to the embarrassed statesmen of Europe that the Swiss treaties of recruitment, even when they favored only one of the belligerents, were not inconsistent with neutrality; at the same time he declared them to be necessary for the neutral Swiss people because by soldiering in foreign service they learned the useful art of war. Nevertheless he felt obliged to lay stress on the fact that the Swiss as a rule only granted permission for enlistment in the case of defensive wars and that it was accidentally forbidden to the recruited troops to fight against the emperor. These excuses show that Vatel, like Grotius, was not free from medieval reminiscences. The allusion to defensive wars marks a revival of Grotius' doctrine of a just war and coincides with this doctrine even in the assumption that a war may be just for both belligerent parties. Grotius had made a point of the rule that a neutral is in duty bound to do nothing in favor of a belligerent who fights for an unjust cause, and on the other hand, not to impede the action of the party that wages a just war. There has been mentioned in one of last week's conferences a dispute that arose about 1780 between Great Britain and the Netherlands concerning the question whether the Dutch were by treaty bound to help the British in a war against France. The States-General refused to send their ships and remained neutral,

arguing that they doubted whether the war waged
by Great Britain was a just war. This answer is
quite in the spirit of Grotius.

The British rulers themselves, from the time of
Queen Elizabeth until the end of the eighteenth century, used to be very liberal in the conception of their
neutrality, sending not only subsidies but also troops
to the enemies of Powers with which they were on
neutral terms or joined by treaties of amity. One
of the most extraordinary examples of unneutral assistance in modern history is the common attitude of
Great Britain and the Netherlands in the War of the
Austrian Succession. Both had by treaties with Austria engaged to guarantee the succession of Maria
Theresa. When she went to war with France, England and Holland provided her with troops and
money. An armed force was dispatched into Germany and gained, under the command of the British
king, a victory over the French forces at Dettingen
in 1743. At that time, both England and Holland
were at peace with France and neutrals in the French
war against Austria. Remarkable as the battle of
Dettingen is as an example of the slow development
of a neutrality law in Europe, it is made more remarkable by the famous *Te Deum* which Handel com-
posed for the victorious king.

No wonder such lax neutrality was, during the
seventeenth and eighteenth centuries, in permanent
danger of being slighted and violated. War was such
a natural state of things, that belligerent parties
naïvely assumed the privilege of taking all measures
necessitated by the aims of the war even when they
were most obnoxious to neutral states. Grotius allows in cases of necessity the passage of belligerent

troops across neutral territory, citing the behavior of Moses marching with the people of Israel through Idumea to Canaan. Naval warfare used to be very disrespectful of the rights and interests of neutrals. During the war between England and France in Europe, and England and the American colonies, 1778–83, the Empress of Russia, Catherine II, organized the so-called armed neutrality, first between Russia, Sweden, and Denmark, later obtaining the adhesion of other Powers, especially Prussia, Austria, and Holland. The armed neutrality was obviously directed against England, whose treatment of neutral commerce during the Seven Years' War, 1756–63, had caused bitter complaints by many European Powers. Such complaints were disregarded by England so long as neutral Powers acted in isolation; for the position of a single neutral Power that wished to avoid a war was weak enough. Now, the armed neutrality could dare to use force in maintaining neutral rights and the Powers set fixed rules whereby these rights were specialized. In doing this they followed not the doctrine of Vatel but of Bynkershoek. As Bynkershoek's statement is the first formulation of modern neutrality, I may be allowed to use it in the translation of Sir Geoffrey Butler:

The justice or injustice of a war does not affect a common friend. It is not for him to place himself as judge between the two belligerents who are, the one and the other, his friends; nor, on the ground that their cause is the more just or less, accord or refuse more or less to this one or that. If I am neither on one side nor the other I cannot aid the one in such a way as will hurt the other.

Starting from the principle of perfect impartiality

of attitude with regard to the belligerent parties, the allied neutrals demanded an equal respect of their rights. The rules they fixed were not officially adopted by belligerents, especially by England, until a much later time; nevertheless they had a great influence on the public opinion of Europe and they were partly sanctioned afterward by the Declaration of Paris and the Hague Neutrality Conventions. I will not go into the detail of these rules, because they are mainly the subject of another course of lectures, on the freedom of the seas.

As a matter of fact, belligerents have never lost the traditional feeling that their interests are more worthy of being maintained than those of neutrals. Especially on the common highway of all nations, the high sea, they claim a privilege for their martial operations. Studying this question, I was always reminded of some fighting scenes of my boyhood. The lower classes of my school lived in an old feud with a public school of my native town in the Rhineland. In winter time we used to fight our battles by snowballing one another, and in view of the *terrain coupé* of the environs, we preferred for that purpose to use the highway. We believed in paying ample regard to the interests of neutral passengers and pedestrians by crying "Attention!" and were very much hurt when the policeman, as a sort of armed neutrality, stopped our battles. I shall add, as a parenthesis, that the public school boys sometimes applied the military device of putting stones into their snowballs; we thought that was bad sport; and we would not have sufficiently appreciated the explanation of the enemy experts that this measure, even if it offended the humanizing tendencies of our time, was

taken in order to shorten the war and to accelerate
the freedom of the highway. Now, what we did in
boyish sport, belligerents are accustomed to do in
bitter earnest, and indeed a nation fighting for its
existence will not easily bow before neutrality rules
of international law even if codified by diplomatic
conferences. I understand that Great Britain during
the World War departed from those rules and developed a new and highly effective system of distant
blockade, adding to such blockade, embargo on neutral ships, extension of the contraband list, declaration of parts of the open sea as a military area, and
so on. She thereby exercised a breath-taking economic pressure on the Central Powers, who, on their
part, equally left the paths of legal sea warfare
marked by the London Conference of 1909. As usual,
every belligerent party, to mollify the exasperation
of the neutrals, and probably in good faith, pretended that it was only replying to the illegal measures of the enemy. As a judicial adviser of the German Foreign Office, especially on questions of sea
warfare and economic war, I watched very closely
the development of that new form of blockade. At
the beginning, I had hoped that British Admiralty
Courts would restrict the action of the naval forces,
especially after the sentence in the Zamora case;
afterward when British Prize Courts renounced judicial control over Orders in Council as to their consistency with the Law of Nations, I set my hope on a
combined action of the neutrals of which the United
States would take the lead. Such hope was in some
measure justified by the note of State Secretary
Lansing of November, 1915, enumerating the hun-
dreds of cases where Great Britain, in the opinion

of the Government of the United States, had by her
naval warfare infringed the neutral rights of that
country. But the British Government succeeded in a
masterly way, by setting up an unparalleled control-
ling organization, to hush the protestations of the
neutrals and to include their territories in the system of the economic blockade. I quite agree with
what has been said during the lecture courses of this
term about the right of each sovereign Power to
decide on the importation or exportation of goods
into or from her territory, and about the right of
each belligerent Power to make agreements with
neutral merchants concerning such imports or ex-
ports; but I beg to state that neither neutral Powers
nor neutral merchants would have been found ready
to enter into such agreements if the sea power of
Great Britain had not been ready to do the utmost
damage possible to neutral commerce in case such
agreements should not be reached. When the *Société Suisse de Surveillance Economique,* the famous
S.S.S., had begun to operate, I paid a short visit
to Switzerland and found out that the Swiss were
not at all pleased with the system. They translated
the S.S.S. by the words *Souveraineté Suisse sus-
pendue*—Swiss sovereignty suspended. The feeling
of an affront offered to the sovereignty of neutral
Powers by both belligerent parties—against Germany it was raised by the effects of submarine warfare—was widespread throughout the neutral world.
But it was a world diminishing from year to year.
Neutrality lost its meaning in a war waged by a big
coalition of peoples against a small one and with
very different principles on both sides. I do not wish
to speak about the motives or aims of the monarchs,

governments, generals, and admirals concerned in the Great War, much less to judge their actions; but speaking of the man in the street and of the rank and file, I venture to suggest that the allied and associated peoples fought for democracy (including even the Russian czar) against imperialism and militarism, the German people in defense of the *Reich* against the policy of encircling Germany. The good faith of all peoples involved in this greatest civil war of the white race is the most tragic aspect of the enormous sacrifices it demanded from victorious and vanquished, from belligerent and neutral nations alike. This being so, it is easy to understand that the Allied Powers saw in the neutral attitude of nations somewhat dependent on their good will a sort of felony; the old idea of *bellum justum,* of the legal obligations that the neutrals have to a just belligerent, was revived during the War. We find its conventional sanction in Article 16 of the Covenant of the League of Nations. I shall mention the provisions of Article 16 afterward; what I wish to make quite clear now is that this Article, by combining the use of armed forces of League members with their economic pressure upon a recalcitrant state, legalizes in international practice the system introduced by Great Britain and her allies during the Great War. Undoubtedly, that system applied in a League war will produce the same effects upon neutral interests as it did during the war of 1914–18. But President Wilson was right, generally speaking, when he, embarking for the Paris Peace Conference on the *George Washington,* expressed the conviction that neutrality will not subsist in a universal League of Nations. He only overlooked that gap in the Covenant which I

mentioned in my second lecture, Article 15, leaving a
member of the League free to fight out its quarrel
with another member when all peaceful means of
deciding it provided in Articles 12 to 15 of the Covenant had failed. President Wilson, furthermore, did
not foresee that the League would in such a measure
lack universality.

Now I venture to say that the practice of distant
economic blockade, introduced by Great Britain and
her allies into the international practice of warfare,
will not be a good precedent making international
law in wars that are now called private wars; that
is, wars waged in accordance with Article 15 of the
Covenant, between two members of the League or,
according to Article 17, between a member state
and a non-member state. In these cases, the question
of applying the precedents of the World War or the
rules of the Paris Declaration of 1856, the Hague
Conventions of 1907, or even the unratified Articles
of the London Declaration of 1909, would rather be
settled by the distribution of sea power between the
belligerent parties and the neutrals than by precedents. You know, in these cases, there will be a real
neutrality under the Covenant. If, for example (I
am now referring not to probabilities, hardly to possibilities), in a war between France and Italy that
could not be avoided by means of the Covenant, the
United States and Great Britain should remain neutral, I do not believe that they would consent to a
blockade practice modeled after the pattern of the
Great War, whereby France might try to prevent
Italy from getting ammunition and food over her
land frontiers. The attempt in itself seems to me not
wholly without prospect of success in view of French

naval, political, and economic power and the proportional weakness of those neighbor states whose export goods Italy would wish to acquire, including Germany and Czechoslovakia.

If, on the other hand, there should be a war between Great Britain and Russia after the failure of the proceedings of the League, provided in Article 17 of the Covenant, Great Britain would possibly, besides waging a normal war on land to defend her Indian Empire, and carrying on a normal blockade of the Baltic Coast of Russia or the White Sea, adopt the same methods of distant economic blockade as in the Great War, in order to interrupt and stop all exportation to Russia across Scandinavia and the Baltic states, central Europe, Turkey, and Persia. The United States would undoubtedly be very much hampered in their trade by such a policy; but they might acquiesce in it as they acquiesced in the corresponding measures taken by the Allies during the Great War, and as Great Britain acquiesced in the blockade and contraband practice of the northern states, especially in the doctrine of American Prize Courts on continuous voyage, during the Civil War.

If it is really the right time for trying a new codification of the Law of Neutrality, the delegates of the interested Powers should bear in mind that possibly the rules destined for a lawful private war, the war of a single state against a single state under the Covenant, should be different from those destined for a League war of execution or sanction, and we, therefore, are obliged to go back from the doctrine of Bynkershoek to the doctrine of Grotius.

As to such a war of sanction, I have one remark to offer regarding the binding force of some proposals the Council of the League is authorized to make under Article 16 of the Covenant. It can, in fact, fix the contributions each individual member has to make of his own land, naval, and air forces to such a joint action of the League.

In the Covenant there is no special provision fixing the method by which the League arrives at a resolution to begin an executory war against a member; the Protocol of Geneva has tried to fill up this gap, but it has not been ratified and I doubt if ever the British Dominions will accept a similar proposal. Therefore, I presume that every member of the League, not only the members of the Council, has an equal right to decide if an executory war is called for and if it has to follow the proposals of the Council. When Germany concluded the Locarno Treaties with Great Britain, France, Belgium, and Italy and the Arbitration Treaties with Poland and Czechoslovakia in 1925 as a preliminary to Germany's entry into the League of Nations, the German Government wished to make clear that Germany's position as a state in the center of Europe, and as a disarmed state, would make it very difficult for her to let League troops march through her territory and to send part of her own armed forces to join the forces of the League. A disarmed nation, compelled to give up neutrality, has more to fear from the revenge of a belligerent, who has had grounds to count on her neutrality, than a strong military Power. And it may be recalled that the German people have experienced in former centuries the disadvantages of a geographical situation that made their territory one of the most sanguinary battlefields of Europe. This was the reason why the German Government stated in a note of October 16, 1925, that Germany, by entering into the League of Nations, could take upon herself the obligations viewed in Article 16 of the Covenant, only within the measure prescribed by her geographic and military situations; and the other contracting parties of the Locarno Treaties answered by corresponding, if more cautiously formulated, notes. In my opinion, the statement of the German Government holds good for every member of the League; should the United States join the League, I am sure they will take the same attitude, and I may refer in this connection to a statement State Secretary Kellogg made in April, 1928, in an address before the American Society of International Law. Mr. Kellogg said: "The League Covenant imposed no affirmative primary obligation to go to war. It might authorize a war, but each member would decide for itself what was aggression and what was defense."

From what I have tried to explain of the working out of the Covenant and the Pact of Locarno, it seems to follow that President Wilson's statement was not correct concerning the future vanishing of the international legal notion of neutrality. On the contrary, the Versailles Treaty so intimately connected with the Covenant of the League provides a special form of neutrality—the neutrality not as a right of choice between war and peace but as an international obligation. I have mentioned the resolution of the Swiss cantons in 1638 and acknowledged by international agreement at the Vienna Conference of 1815; this was a permanent, but a freely chosen, neutrality. Switzerland would not have violated the Law of Nations if she had chosen to join one of the belligerent parties during the Great War; she only would have lost once for all the guaranties given her by the Treaty of Vienna. With Belgium it had been different. The southern part of the Netherlands had freed themselves from Holland by the Brussels Revolution of 1830. This territory having been much disputed among the Great Powers since the Middle Ages, the neighbors of Belgium agreed to make her independent, but neutral in the strictest sense of the word; that is to say, Belgium got not only the right of neutrality, but also the obligation to keep neutral. Before the World War, the Great Powers of Europe and the United States of America tried to give a similar constitutional form of permanent neutrality to the Spitzberg Islands in the Arctic Sea where the only settlement worth speaking of, Longyear City, was owned by an American citizen, Mr. Longyear, and his companions. The attempt was frustrated by the outbreak of the War. You all know the neutralization rules agreed upon between the United States and Great Britain with regard to the Panama Canal; similar rules, but farther reaching ones, are made for the Suez Canal, the empire road of Great Britain, and I could deliver many lectures telling of the vicissitudes of the neutralization treaties concerning the straits of the Dardanelles and the Bosporus. Now, the Versailles Treaty, you know, has several articles neutralizing parts of Germany; in a certain area of the Rhineland, on both banks of the Rhine, Germany is prohibited from maintaining armed forces or from erecting fortifications of any kind, and the Kiel Canal between the German Sea and the Baltic Sea, is declared permanently neutral, not to be fortified, and to be free for the passage of merchant ships and warships of all nations at peace with Germany.

The last-named clause of the Versailles Treaty has been the cause of raising a question of neutrality very difficult to decide. I am referring to the *Wimbledon* case, the first case on which the Permanent Court of International Justice in The Hague gave sentence. For those of my hearers who are not intimately acquainted with the activity of the Hague Court, I may be allowed to go a little into the detail of the case, because it is connected with some important problems of neutrality under the Covenant and the Versailles Treaty.

The *Wimbledon* was a British merchant ship, chartered by a French company to carry ammunition from a French port to Danzig during the war between Russia and Poland in 1920. The ammunition was destined for the use of the Polish army; the port of Danzig is virtually a Polish port, because under the Versailles Treaty, Poland is entitled to use the port for her own purposes. I was at that time German Minister of Foreign Affairs; the war between Russia and Poland had given much trouble to the German Government, because we had just by heavy fighting succeeded in subduing dangerous communist rebellions in Saxony and Westfalia, and we knew quite well that a great part of our laboring classes were in favor of Russia. On the other hand, we were pressed very hard by the Allies to reduce our troops even more and we had an intimation from their side that we should let the Haller army, the Polish troops that had served against Germany in France, and some French auxiliaries, march through our country to the battlefields. So I proposed to President Ebert to publish a formal declaration of neutrality with regard to the war between Russia and Poland, claiming the rights and taking the duties of a neutral. The President accepted my proposal and acted on it. The declaration contained a clause forbidding all German citizens to give unneutral assistance to any of the belligerent parties. At that moment, I got a telegram from the authorities in charge of the Kiel Canal that the *Wimbledon,* with her contraband cargo, had entered the Kiel Canal. I instantly ordered her to stop and take the way round Denmark. In spite of the protestations of the Powers concerned, especially Great Britain and France, I insisted on my order, basing it on the neutrality rules of the Law of Nations and appealing to an article of the Versailles Treaty whereby it is provided that all differences arising out of the application or interpretation of the canal clauses shall be decided by arbitration. At last, the Allies consented to that appeal; the *Wimbledon* took her way north, rounding Cape Skagen and losing a dozen days by her stay and the roundabout voyage. When the Permanent Court of International Justice came into function at The Hague, Great Britain, France, Italy, and Poland filed an action against Germany claiming the acknowledgment of the right of the *Wimbledon* to use the Kiel Canal and the payment of damages. After long and interesting pleading the Court gave sentence for the claimants; but three of the members dissented, namely, Professor Schuecking of Kiel, member *ad hoc* for Germany, and the former and the present President of the Court, Professor Huber of Zurich, now President of the International Red Cross Commission in Geneva, and Professor Auzilotti, the

famous Italian author on international law. The
sentence was based on two points: First—a verbal
interpretation of the words "open at every time,"
toujours ouvert, applied also at a time of war and
therefore giving to all treaty rights precedence of
neutrality obligations; second, on a comparison with
precedents regarding the Straits and the Suez and
Panama canals. The dissenting members pointed out
that the treaty clause only envisaged a wartime when
Germany was a belligerent and not a time when she
was neutral; that the special rules concerning other
canals or channels could not be applied to the Kiel
Canal and that therefore Germany was free to apply
the ordinary rules of neutrality to the Kiel Canal.
You will not be surprised to hear that I likewise
dissented from the sentence of the Court, because I
personally am the losing party. The loss is only a
moral and political one, because the German Government was kind enough not to make me pay the
huge sum of damages the Court had fixed as Germany's due. Nevertheless, I must confess that I cannot be quite impartial in this case. What strikes me
most is the fact that neither the majority of the Court
nor the dissenting members seem to have grasped the
decisive argument. The claim and the sentence alike
are based on the Versailles Treaty and presume that
its special clauses are superseding the general rules
of the Law of Nations concerning the rights and
duties of neutrals. Now, Russia is not a party to the
Versailles Treaty, but has always protested against
it in a most energetic way. According to a well-
known rule of international law, a treaty clause does
not hold in an international situation, causing a
justiciable difference, if any of the Powers concerned

are not a party to the treaty. Had I allowed the *Wimbledon* to pass through the Kiel Canal and to bring the ammunition a week or so earlier to the Polish army, Russia would have been justified in claiming satisfaction from Germany for this un-neutral act. I would have pleaded in vain the canal clause of the Versailles Treaty; Russia would have retorted that was no concern of hers, but a *res inter alias acta*—"a matter for somebody else." More-over, I am quite certain that the result of my bowing before the protestations of the Allies would have been to start fresh communist upheavals in Ger-many. Therefore, with all the esteem and respect I feel for the authority of the Hague Court, I have, from every point of view, that of foreign affairs, of domestic policy, and of international public law, a fairly good conscience in dissenting from this sen-tence in the *Wimbledon* case.

The position of Russia in view of the Versailles Treaty and the Covenant brings to mind another question which I shall try to answer in concluding my third lecture. Both Russia and the United States, not being members of the League, have signed the Paris Pact. Does the Pact change the rules concern-ing neutrality? If so, do the changes differ for bellig-erents or neutrals that are not League members? The Pact is a general renunciation of war as a means of national policy; Powers ratifying the Pact will be in duty bound to have no war between them, what-ever may be the character and importance of their differences arising out of conflicting interests or dis-puted rights. If all states of the world were parties to the Pact and if they acted always in conformity with the Pact, there would be no neutrality, because there would be no war; for neutrality, as I stated in beginning my lecture, is a corollary to war. The Pact therefore obliterates the special rules of the Covenant leaving room for neutrality; the Pact rules them out. But, in my opinion, until now the Pact is more of a program than of a contract, more of a promise than of an engagement, more of a hope than of a guaranty. The reservations many Powers have added to their signatures (Germany has made none) seem to me as many back doors for the god Mars to enter again the Palace of Peace after he had been turned out of the front door. Therefore, I cannot oppose the proposal to re-found the International Law of Neutrality that has lost its accepted form in the crucible of the Great War; but besides the advice I ventured to hint respecting the difference between neutrality in a private and a public war, a single states war and a League war, I beg to express my fervent wish that international lawyers, in formulating rules for neutrality, may be anxious to avert making excuses for war. In fact, generally, I am not a great friend of international codification work; in international as in national law, I prefer common law and case law to statute law; but to get case law concerning neutrality, we must first get war, and I hope that I myself and my children will never have this opportunity.

IV

STATE RESPONSIBILITY AND INTERVENTION

In my first lecture I tried to show how the fundamental idea of international public law, the idea of a sovereign state, has developed in Europe since Grotius; in the second and third lectures, I treated the most characteristic attributes of sovereignty as conceived during the last centuries, the right of waging war or remaining neutral under the Law of Nations, the *jus belli ac pacis*. Now we come to a chapter that in itself seems inconsistent with sovereignty, the chapter of state responsibility. Is not that a contradiction in itself? If the essence of statehood is sovereign might, how can a state be responsible to anything outside itself? Who can make a sovereign responsible? The state itself, as owning the supreme *potestas,* the highest jurisdiction, is sole judge over the acts of state.

That indeed was the meaning of the Maxim Marsilius of Padua in the time of the early Renaissance, dug out of the antique system of imperial Rome, the maxim: *Princeps legibus solutus*—"the sovereign is bound by no law." The English version of that maxim is well known; it runs: "The king can do no wrong." It seems to be the rule of reckless absolutism; but in reality it is the exact formula for that strict doctrine of sovereignty that pervades not only the centuries of primitive or enlightened absolutism, but also the nationalism of the nineteenth and even the twentieth century. With such a doctrine, Law of Nations is a fiction; a nation can only be bound by

its own will, in other words, the state, the organized
nation, cannot be bound at all, because it may change
its will according to its own constitution and discretion. International public and private law are therefore, in the meaning of this doctrine of sovereignty,
most clearly defined by Professor Hans Kelsen of
Vienna, who says that it is really not international
but national law, a national law deciding sovereignly
and without an appeal to any authority whatsoever,
on all international questions. Viewed from this an-
gle, an old principle of the common law wins quite a
new meaning. Famous English judges have coined
the legal principle that the Law of Nations is part of
the municipal law of England. The original meaning
is this, that if a court has been convinced that a certain rule is recognized as binding under the Law of
Nations, the court is bound likewise to apply it under
the law of England. In the same sense, Article 4 of
the Weimar Constitution, which I cited in a former
lecture, saying that recognized rules of the Law of
Nations are a binding part of German law, must be
construed. But in the meaning of the strict doctrine
of sovereignty, that principle will say: There is no
Law of Nations outside the law of England; municipal law alone creates international law and makes
it binding on the domestic courts. According to this
doctrine of nationalism even treaty law is, in fact,
national law. What makes a treaty binding is the
ratification of the sovereign, commanding the state
authorities to act on it, not the stipulation or promise
made to another state and accepted by it. The old
rule: *pacta sunt servanda*—"treaties must be kept"
—is, applied to international treaties, a rule of pru-
dence, not of law; it depends on the circumstances,

whether the state shall stick to its will expressed by the treaty or change it. I heartily disagree with this doctrine and likewise with the corresponding practice; both may be stigmatized as Machiavellian. There is a law above the nations even when there is no supernational legislator, a law indeed that is in the making and therefore uncertain, but nevertheless a law, like the early law of most Teutonic nations that was a customary and judge-made law applied a very long time before the customs and sentences were collected by a private codificator or even converted into official statute law. Customs and sentences and statutes are themselves like saplings or suckers, sprouting out of a deep, common rootstock, the underlying primordial law of human nature ruling all sorts and conditions of men living together, working together, struggling and quarreling with each other, from the nomad family to the League of Nations. I do not wish here to philosophize on behalf of Grotius' doctrine on *jus naturale* and *voluntarium,* or *jus gentium,* nor to interfere in the conflict between the naturalist and positivist school of his followers. I will only ask where you find the standard to decide whether an international treaty is a just and equitable one if there is no international law but only treaty law? There must be a higher law behind the treaty to judge it. And where do you take the primordial rule that international treaties ought to be kept but from that higher law? Indeed it is a law without a legislator and without an executor; such law has existed in all ages and with all peoples, and it exists today in the most civilized countries, a law in being before it is found out by the judge or the legislator and enforced by the bailiff. It is this law that makes sovereign states responsible. Law in the last instance does not derive its authority from the state, but from God who made mankind to strive after the righteousness of his kingdom.

In my first lecture I tried to show the double limits of sovereignty, the inward limit where state power crashed against individual liberty, against the inborn rights of a man and a citizen, and the outward limit where the right of a sovereign state meets with the equal rights of other states. In trespassing those limits, the state assumes a double burden of responsibility; in the former case, that of crossing the limits of inward power, the state is, according to modern constitutional law, responsible before its own courts and authorities; in the latter case, the transgression of the limits of outward power, it may be made responsible before an international authority, for instance a court of arbitration or international justice, before the public opinion of the civilized world, or— as a judgment of last resort—before the ordeal of war. I shall consider the inward responsibility first; it has not only a domestic but also an international aspect, as we shall see hereafter.

In the era of feudalism, the connection of a European prince claiming the *suprema potestas,* the sovereignty over his land, with the inhabitants of that land was in most cases not a direct one but broken by many intermediate dependencies of vassalage. At the same time, the field of governmental activities that rulers of that era contemplated as being within the scope of their official duties was very small indeed, in comparison with modern state socialism and state guardianship. It is, therefore, not strange that in Europe the first bill of rights was enforced not in favor of the commoners' liberties but in favor of the privileges of barons. The Magna Charta of England makes the king responsible to his barons, not the Government responsible to Parliament. The idea was very far from the public opinion of feudal times that every subject has an enforceable claim against his own sovereign in case an official of that sovereign, or the government, or the sovereign himself committed an unjust act to that subject's detriment, or in case they have failed in fulfilling a contractual obligation incurred in his favor. In the era of enlightened absolutism, the courts of justice, and the lawyers of the crown, adopted the old Roman doctrine of the *Fiscus* or Exchequer being the substitute of the sovereign prince in such civil cases where it seemed just and equitable that the prince should be sued in courts of justice like a private person, and sentenced to pay what the court would find the prince owed to his subject. Such an infringement on sovereignty, a system splitting sovereignty into two parts, which seems quite obvious and natural to modern European aspects of constitutional law, was rather a novelty in Grotius' time.

The conservatism of English law and the reverence English courts have always manifested for the sovereign rights and prerogatives of the English Crown show that the old idea has not yet quite vanished in that country. I may be justified in making this statement by an experience I had in 1905 regarding the English law on state responsibility. In that year, the German Government prepared a bill to be introduced in the *Reichstag* and providing certain rules of liability to be assumed by the *Reich* on behalf of damages inflicted on private persons by faulty

or culpable actions of its functionaries. In view of
this bill, the Board of the *Deutsche Juristentag,* the
General Conference of German and Austrian jurists,
who for fifty years have done good service for the
parliamentary committees in doing scientific preparatory work for legislation, asked me to deliver a
report on the bill as to its advisability and to the
soundness of its planned special rules. I was then a
member of the Court of Appeal in Kiel and I wished
to compare continental law, especially German and
French law, which I knew fairly well, with English
law, which it was very difficult then to study in Germany. So I came to London and had the privilege,
through the kindness of a well-known member of the
London Bar, to study the problem of civil responsibility of the state in Lincoln's Inn Library. There I
found out that in the first place the Exchequer refused under English law any liability for damages
resulting from so-called "acts of state," political
acts falling under the discretion of the Government,
and secondly, that in other cases no action against
the Crown of England or her representative authorities would lie in an English court before a petition
was presented asking the king to allow the petitioner
to file the action, and before the answer was given on
behalf of the king: "Let right be done." I was then,
and I have always been, a great partisan of a strong
executive power by the side of constitutional guaranty for individual freedom (an independent judiciary) ; so the English system impressed me strongly.
Before I could deliver my report before the *Juristentag* (my co-reporter would have been Otto von
Gierke, who supported the plan of the Government
with all his ability) I was appointed a councilor of

the Imperial Ministry of Justice, and it befell me
to defend before the *Reichstag* the bill which I had
made up my mind to oppose before the *Juristentag*.
That was my first experience of the essential change
I had undergone when I had ceased to be a judge and
had begun to be an administrative functionary. As a
judge, I knew no guiding star but my conviction; as
a particle of a big administration, I had to advocate
the views of my superiors. I did my duty and the bill
went through in 1906. It is in force now, although
partly replaced by an article of our Weimar Constitution (Article 139) which contains the following
provisions: If a functionary, in the exercise of public
authority vested in him, violates an official duty incumbent on him not as against the state but as
against a third party, the state to whose service the
functionary is appointed shall be held responsible;
and the claim of the injured party may be filed before the courts of common law. This Article applies
also to functionaries of the *Reich* making the *Reich*
liable. But according to several sentences of the
German Supreme Court, the general principle sanctioned by the Weimar Constitution does not exclude
or repeal the special provisos contained in the Liability Act of 1906. Two of these provisos are important for the argument of my lecture today, and I beg
to cite them as an explanation of my telling you so
much about German law regarding state responsibility.

The first proviso says that a suit against the *Reich*
based on the Liability Act and filed by a foreigner
shall not lie, unless the court that has jurisdiction in
the case has been convinced by information given by
the German Foreign Office that the state of which

that foreigner is a national accords to a German citizen a corresponding claim. A British subject contending that he is injured by the official action of a functionary of the *Reich* and wishing to file against the *Reich* a suit for damages must first prove to the satisfaction of the Foreign Office that an English court would, in a similar case, grant an action to a German claimant. I am not sure what attitude the Foreign Office of the *Reich* would take now in such an action. To be sure, the answers regarding the different liability laws of civilized states would not show a general principle of international law, but a great variety of national solutions.

The second proviso of our German Special Law on State Responsibility purports that in a case of foreign policy, if it is contended that a representative of the *Reich* in a foreign country, an ambassador or minister plenipotentiary or another functionary of the administration of Germany's foreign affairs, has violated the official duties incumbent on him as against a third party, the action shall be dismissed if the Minister of Foreign Affairs, informed of the action, states that the measure taken by the functionary was an act necessitated by the political interests of the *Reich* or, according to the English term, an act of state.

In defending these two provisos before the *Reichstag* I could make use of what I had learned in the Lincoln's Inn Library and I felt no strain on my conscience. The provisos show that the inward liability which a state assumes in transgressing the limits of its sovereign power may be of international importance. The transgression is very often an *ultra vires* act of a public functionary; when a foreigner is injured by such an act, the state, whose national he is, may claim damages for him through diplomatic channels. It is a general practice, almost a universally accepted rule of the Law of Nations, that the defendant state is always justified in rejecting the claim when the private party concerned did not try the judicial way opened to him by the municipal law of that state, if necessary even to the court of last resort. I am not quite sure if this rule will be generally and permanently acknowledged in the future; what strikes me in pondering over the problem is this: Many claims of that sort have, after unsuccessful diplomatic negotiations, been brought before an international court of arbitration or a court of international justice. Now I think I am right in supposing that a sovereign state will be more ready to take the way of arbitration after its diplomats have failed to attain a success or a compromise in the disputed matter, than after a sentence of the supreme court of its country has dismissed the foreign claim. The great jurist and statesman of the United States, Mr. Root, seems to be of the same opinion. In an address he delivered as President of the American Society of International Law, Secretary of State Root said he thought it rather dangerous to refer international claims of this sort generally to the municipal courts before dealing with them by diplomacy or arbitration, because it was irritating and harmful to a conciliatory procedure when the national court of last resort had dismissed a private action and the claim of the foreign state had to be based on an attack against the correctness or impartiality of the national judiciary. But that remark of Mr. Root, well founded in international psychology as I think it, is a single voice, a *hapax eiremenon* as the Greeks used to say, and the arbitration treaties of many nations, for instance the treaty between Germany and Switzerland of which I drew the outlines with Professor Huber in 1921, contain that clause of preliminary private action. The only exception to this clause is the case of denied justice, the case when courts have refused to hear the injured foreigner.

In Grotius' time, such a responsibility of the state was scarcely conceived at all. Neither was a sovereign to be sued before his own courts, nor could a private individual hope to get redress for injuries committed by foreign authorities, before a foreign court. In my second lecture I remarked that at the end of the Middle Ages it was not the sovereign who was made responsible for the committals of his subjects, but the subjects were made responsible for the committals of their sovereign or their countrymen, and I sketched the form wherein that responsibility was enforced until the eighteenth century, the form of private reprisals. Making by private armed force an innocent member of a foreign nation pay for what a guilty one has committed, is an old-fashioned consequence of that primordial national solidarity that seemed forgotten in the time of absolutism but which was revived during the Great War and has found its sanction under international law by the peace treaties, especially by their economic clauses.

Taking the practice of reprisals into their own hands, the sovereigns of Europe gave to the claims of their injured subjects quite another character. The injustice shown against the subjects by private foreigners or foreign authorities appeared as an affront put upon the dignity of their sovereigns. The difference between such cases of an indirect violation of international law and a direct delictual action of one state against another state is, in its practical consequences, of no great account, especially as to the means of getting redress by apology, payment of damages, reparation, and other satisfaction given to the claimant state by the defendant state. But different forms of international action have been used as a private claim law at the bottom of a diplomatic remonstration, or a violation of rights of the remonstrating state itself. It is only to the former category that the doctrine of so-called reclamations is applicable.

I will not go into the details of this most technical and complicated matter; it would be worth while to discuss it at a round table through a whole term of the Williamstown Institute of Politics. Many instances of state responsibility are collected in such standard works of American authors on international law as Mr. John Bassett Moore's *Digest of International Law,* Volume VI, and Professor Edwin M. Borchard's book concerning the diplomatic protection of citizens abroad. A most comprehensive study of the whole matter may be found in the excellent research work conducted by a special committee at Harvard under the direction of Professor Manley O. Hudson, with the assistance of Mr. Richard W. Flournoy, Professor Edwin M. Borchard, and Professor George Grafton Wilson. I feel bound to express not only my personal gratitude, as a professor of international law at a German university, for the unparalleled contribution American writers on state responsibility have made, a contribution which has led to a quicker development of international public law in Europe, but also my great disappointment that this splendid work, though fully recognized by the League of Nations and by the Codification Conference assembled at The Hague in March and April of this year, did not succeed in helping to a common acceptance either of the rules proposed by the American research committee or of the proposals that the League of Nations Committee has offered to that conference as bases of discussion.

The greatest difficulties in the matter of state liability arise when the state that is held responsible for an act violating the Law of Nations has been involved in a revolution or civil war, or if that state is constitutionally not a unit but a federation of units, of which only one is in default. To speak first of this second case, you all know the difficulties that arose between the Government of the United States and other nations on behalf of the so-called Georgia claims after the Civil War, or between the United States and Japan on behalf of some statutes of the state of California. In Germany or Switzerland, similar cases are possible; but the constitutions of both countries would, in my opinion, exclude an exception made by the Federal Government against the claim of a foreign state and based on the reason that the contractual or delictual liability lay with a single land or canton and not with the Union, the *Reich*, or the *Bund*. For by an express article of the Weimar Constitution the *Reich* has to represent the states or *Laender* as against a foreign state, and as far as my knowledge of the Swiss Constitution goes, the same rule applies to the relation of the *Bund* and the cantons respecting liabilities under the Law of Nations.

A similar difficulty arises by another form of splitting the sovereignty: The adoption of Montesquieu's
doctrine of division of powers. If the executive has
violated the Law of Nations, there is no doubt that
the state is in duty bound and practically able to
offer redress; but, if the claim of the foreign state
concerns an act of parliament or a sentence of the
judiciary, the case is far more complicated. The executive, even if he is convinced of the justice of a
foreign claim and the responsibility of his own state,
will under the constitutional system of the greater
part of modern civilized nations be unable to compel
a parliament to change a statute whereby an international obligation of that state has been violated or
to prevent a parliament from passing such a statute.
And in the same way he will find it impossible to
change the opinion of a supreme court which has
given sentence in opposition to a claim that the government has deemed justified under international
law. The relation between national and international
jurisdiction is one of the most difficult problems of
our time and has caused a very spirited discussion
at the last conference of the Institute of International Law held at New York in October and at the
Hague Codification Conference.

But the most difficult problem of state responsibility is that emerging from a revolution or a civil
war. In countries where they are most frequent there
is also the greatest negligence in discriminating between the opposite party and the peaceable and neutral foreigners, and, therefore, volumes have been
written on the question of the liability of states due
to damages done to foreigners during a revolution.
It is all right to base such a claim on the rules of

international law concerning state responsibility; but who is representing the state on this occasion? That is the question. Let us assume, for instance, that a revolutionary party has done reckless injury to foreigners and has been defeated afterward; you cannot get redress from that party because it is defeated, and if you address your claim to the victorious government, it will object *force majeure.* Take the opposite case: The government, threatened by a revolution, takes forced loans or unjust requisitions from foreign firms and is afterward overthrown. Can you sue victorious rebels for damages on behalf of the violations of international law committed by a tyrannical government they have defeated? This exception resembles that of the Soviet Government concerning some international obligations incurred by the Czar's government. In such cases, the rule of international law that changes of government will not change foreign liabilities of the state, is not absolutely applicable. You see, the failure of the last Hague Conference is not due to the ill-will of the delegates assembled, or of the governments that appointed them, but to the intrinsic difficulties of the matter, especially in cases of a divided or split sovereignty of the responsible state, and to the great difference of the interests which the nations concerned are eager to maintain.

I now come to a short survey of the means whereby the responsibility of a state if justly asserted by another state may be enforced under the Law of Nations. I mentioned four: diplomatic negotiations, arbitration, reprisals, war. As a conclusion of my fourth lecture I wish to say a little more about a very customary fifth means, called intervention.

Now intervention, in modern international law, has more than one meaning, and much confusion has arisen by using the term "intervention" in various senses at the same time. In the first instance, intervention may mean a political action intended to decide an international contest between two other states, in the interest of universal peace; secondly, it may mean an action interfering with the domestic struggles of one other state; and lastly, the word "intervention" is applied to those political acts whereby a state tries to enforce a claim that one of its subjects or citizens is justified in raising against another state because of a violation of international law. By this sort of intervention the state whose national is injured in most cases applies force short of war. The first category of intervention is one of the means a neutral state may use to bring a difference between two or more other states to an end; those means are good offices, mediation, or intervention. In offering her good offices to the parties of an international strife, the neutral Power is absolutely impartial, she disclaims any selfish interest, she makes no specific proposal, but she declares her readiness to be the messenger of any proposals one party wishes to make to the other in the common interest of peace. This was the position Bismarck adopted when he proposed the Berlin Conference of 1878 after the war between Russia and Turkey in view of the imminent danger of a rupture between Russia and Great Britain caused by the preliminary Treaty of San Stefano. In his famous speech before the *Diet* he told the members of Parliament that his aim was nothing else than to play the rôle of an honest broker who brings the two parties of a business together. His brokerage was the bad humor of both parties. A dozen years before, at the end of the war between Prussia and Austria, Napoleon III offered his good offices to both parties, but Bismarck, doubting the impartiality of the broker, preferred to hasten the immediate peace negotiations so that he was able to spare the brokerage. Napoleon was very much annoyed at losing the opportunity of a political gain and tried to retrieve it afterward by negotiations concerning Luxemburg and Belgium; but Bismarck put him off until 1870 when he published in the *London Times* a facsimile of the French proposal about Belgium and secured thereby Great Britain's neutrality in the war against France.

Mediation is a stronger method of bringing together parties in dispute. A mediator is also bound to be impartial and to address himself to both quarreling parties alike. But generally he makes certain proposals for settling the matter and may thereby take care of his own interests. That was the position of Great Britain when she settled the difference that arose between France and Prussia over the Grand Duchy of Luxemburg. Luxemburg was a member of the German Confederation, but Prussia had the right of maintaining a garrison in the stronghold of its capital. After the war between Prussia and Austria and the dissolution of the German Confederation, Napoleon III insisted on the cession of Luxemburg to France as a counterpoise against the greater weight Prussia had won in European politics by her victory over Austria. When Bismarck refused, a war between France and Prussia was already imminent in 1867. Then Great Britain acted as mediator and at the London Conference of that year the dispute was settled by the marching off of the Prussian troops, the razing of the strongholds, and the neutralization of the Luxemburg territory in conformity with British proposals. Another good example of mediation is the action of the United States that led to the Peace of Portsmouth ending the war between Russia and Japan. During the Great War, the move of the Holy See in the summer of 1917 may be conceived as an attempt at mediation.

If mediation is a stronger action than good offices, intervention is stronger than mediation. A neutral Power that intervenes in a quarrel between other Powers throws her political and military forces into one scale of the balance and therefore ceases to be neutral, or she compels both parties to end the quarrel by an agreement that is more or less dictated. Of the latter sort—God Neptune raising his trident and shouting *quos ego*—there are not many examples in the history of European Powers, but some may be cited by an expert in Great Britain's colonial and eastern policy. There was that one-sided and unhappy intervention of Russia, France, and Germany after the war between China and Japan that upset the Peace Treaty of Shimonoseki, and that even more unhappy intervention of Germany when she backed Austria in her difference with Russia about the annexation of Bosnia. The first was a prelude to the Russo-Japanese War of 1904, the second a prelude to the World War. During the Great War, there was the most important intervention in the world's history, that of the United States associating with the Allies against Germany.

Of this sort of intervention there did not exist in Europe, before the Great War, any recognized set

of rules under the Law of Nations; every sovereign
Power, by virtue of her independence and legal
equality, had the faculty of intervention as it had
the right to go to war and to conclude or keep peace.
As you will have remarked by the historical examples
I have given, every action of a state intended to influence a quarrel of two other states, be it good offices,
mediation, or intervention in whatsoever form, may
occur both before and after the outbreak of a war.
The states of Europe have not always been very
cautious in meddling with other peoples' struggles;
nevertheless, even mediation and good offices aroused
in the public opinion of the nations concerned and in
the minds of their leading statesmen, bitter and
angry feelings, as Bismarck found out after the Berlin Conference of 1878, and as Emperor William
found out after Shimonoseki and after the Bosnian
Crisis. Under the Covenant of the League of Nations,
the right of intervention is reserved to the Council of
the League. Under Articles 10, 11, 12, 15, 16, and 17,
in every case of grave differences between members
or non-members of the League the measures necessary for avoiding a rupture between the states concerned or, if that has already taken place, the intervention on behalf of the interests of the League are
to be taken or advised by the Council. There is only
one possibility left for private intervention of this
sort, that is when a private war is justified under
Articles 15 and 17, and the means of peaceable settlement of the dispute have failed. Under the Briand-
Kellogg Pact, intervention is not excluded, but a signatory Power is not allowed to enforce her intervention by beginning or entering a war.

The second category of intervention is intervention in the domestic disputes of another nation. In my first lecture, I spoke of this kind of intervention and I declared as my opinion, that intervention of a foreign Power in the inner affairs of an independent state is the worst affront that can be put upon sovereignty. This affront has been experienced by many European nations during the last four centuries. After the Reformation, one Power intervened in the religious differences of the other, as Sweden and France did in the religious wars of Germany; after the French Revolution, the monarchs of Europe intervened on behalf of the Bourbon dynasty and against the French Republic; after the Napoleonic Wars, the Holy Alliance intervened in many cases on behalf of legitimacy and conservative government against liberalism and democracy, and the Pentarchy of the great European Powers—Russia, Prussia, Austria, Great Britain, and France—intervened on behalf of the maintenance of the European system based on the Vienna peace treaty. In 1821 Austrian troops intervened in the Kingdom of Naples to put down the insurrection against *il Re Bomba,*—"the bomb King," as he was called by his people; and in 1823, French troops marched into Spain to defend, in the name of the Pentarchy, the legitimate dynasty against a dangerous insurrection. During the twenties of the last century, the fetters that had bound Great Britain to the Pentarchy were loosened by the policy of Canning. England reminded herself of her parliamentary system and began to intervene for liberalism and democracy. Such an intervention led to the *untoward event* of the Battle of Navarino where the Turkish fleet was sunk by the British navy in order to help the Greeks fighting for their liberty.

On the contrary, some years before Great Britain had, with armed forces, intervened for Spain and against the insurrection of her South American colonies. When I was in Argentina in 1922, I was shown the locality where a hundred years before a British landing force was beaten by an Argentine army and compelled to retreat to their ships. Interventions of that kind were the cause of President Monroe's immortal declaration of December, 1823. The last attempt of a European Power to intervene in domestic affairs of an American state was that of Napoleon III in favor of Emperor Maximilian of Mexico and against the Republican party under Benito Juarez—the last intervention of this sort and the most tragic.

Under the Covenant of the League such interventions seem to me forbidden by express treaty law. Article 15, Section 8, of the Covenant provides that in any difference which a party member of the League may bring before the Council because it is not brought before a court of international arbitration or jurisdiction, there is a good exception to the claim that the difference relates to a question left exclusively, under the Law of Nations, to the jurisdiction of that member. In case such an exception is made and the Council recognize its correctness, the League itself may not intervene; the Council restrict their action to a report on the exception and do not propose a solution of the difference. Indeed, the Covenant does not say what cases are left to the exclusive jurisdiction of a member; but it is, I think, universally acknowledged that quarrels about constitutional questions, even if they lead to the use of armed force between citizens, fall under that category. Therefore, if even the League refrains from any action in such a case brought before the Council by a member wishing to intervene, I venture to conclude that an individual intervention of any member of the League in like cases is out of the question and would have the character of a hostile act if directed against a *de jure* or a *de facto* government.

Interventions of this sort, supporting one party of a foreign country and weakening the other party, are often mingled with the third and last form of intervention: that of forcible acts short of war against the government of a foreign nation. For many cases of intervention are connected with acts of violence committed by citizens of one state against citizens of a foreign state in time of a revolution, and in holding the party in power responsible for the damage done and intervening against them, the intervening state may bring support to the other party. But in principle there is a difference between an intervention in favor of a national political party and an intervention to enforce a political or justiciable claim against the foreign state as an international unit. Interventions in this category have always, at least in Europe, been recognized as justified under the Law of Nations. They coincide with the modern form of reprisals, taken not against the individual citizens or subjects of a state, but against the state itself. The causes of such an intervention may be manifold: I shall not go into details in this lecture. It may suffice to say that European states intervened not only in cases of international delinquency of a state or of injurious actions committed by authorities for which a state is responsible, but also in cases of purely financial default. As an example of such an intervention I may cite the action of the European creditor Powers against Egypt, Turkey, and Greece. "Creditor Powers" is an incorrect term; for the states concerned were not creditors of the debtor state, but their citizens or subjects were, and the respective states had taken the citizens' claims into their own hands. In former times it was a settled practice of debtor states to give to the creditor state (sometimes it was a rich prince who had lent the money himself) part of the state territory in pledge by a sort of cession. So an old feof of the Holy Roman Empire, the town of Wismar and the surrounding territory, had been ceded by the feoffee, King of Sweden, to the Grand Duke of Mecklenburg as a pledge for a loan of about a million dollars by the Treaty of Malmoe, June, 1803. This territory came definitely under the sovereignty of the new German Empire a hundred years after,—June, 1903,—the Grand Duke of Mecklenburg renouncing his financial claim and Sweden her territorial rights over the pledged territory. In other cases, European Powers obtained security for such financial or economical claims by occupying forcibly a part of the territory of a debtor state. The last and most important example of such an action of getting "productive pledges" was the invasion of the Ruhr district by French and other troops in 1923. Public opinion early began to protest against these measures; as early as 1868, when European Powers began to enforce economic claims of their subjects against sundry states of Latin America, the Argentine international lawyer and author Calvo objected energetically to this practice. Later on, the Argentine Minister of Foreign Affairs, Drago, in a note directed to his representative in Washington, December, 1902, expressed his opinion that to use armed force for such purposes was against the recognized principles of the Law of Nations. At the second Peace Conference at The Hague, 1907, the United States of America supporting the assertion of Minister Drago; a convention— the so-called Drago-Porter Convention—was signed and afterward ratified by many Powers whereby the contracting parties renounced the use of armed force in maintaining contractual obligations claimed by the government of one party against the government of another party, unless the latter government had frustrated an attempt to settle the dispute by arbitration. The United States did not ratify the Drago-Porter Convention without an important reservation. At all events, the Drago doctrine, in my opinion, cannot be considered as a general rule of international law, but only as treaty law. As far as I know, many of the states of Latin America have refused to sign the Convention.

In other cases, European Powers, to enforce fulfilment of treaty obligations or reparations for injustice committed against themselves or against their nationals, have resorted to a specific form of intervention known under the term of pacific blockade. On pacific blockade, volumes have been published. I will only remind my hearers of the pacific blockade resorted to by Great Britain and Germany in 1902 against Venezuela, Italy joining the blockading Powers afterward. The characteristic result of that pacific blockade was the attitude taken by the United States of America. The American Government declared that they did not object to a European state using armed force against a state of South America being in default of its international duties and obligations, but they could not acknowledge a pacific blockade as binding with regard to the commerce of any nation other than those participating in the blockade. According to European precedents, this was a new doctrine; but the blockading Powers in acceding to it, changed the pacific blockade to a war blockade by bombarding Puerto Cabello. The dispute with General Castro, the President of Venezuela, was then settled, you know, by mediation of the United States and by the Arbitration Treaty of Washington followed by a sentence of the Permanent International Court of Arbitration at The Hague.

In summing up, I really think intervention in any form, especially intervention in the domestic affairs of a foreign state, is not only a measure most dangerous for peace in general but contrary to basic principles of international law. The great German philosopher, Immanuel Kant, in his small book on the problem of perpetual peace, formulating some preliminary articles for a universal peace treaty, has drawn up the fifth article as follows:

"No state may intervene forcibly in the constitution or the administration of another state."

I think Kant is right. His principle, however, does not comprehend—at least not in express terms —the case of a common action of a society of states against a member in default of its international obligations; such common action is provided, for example, by the Berlin Treaty of 1878 giving the Great Powers of Europe a right to common intervention against Turkey as a guaranty of the fulfilment of her treaty obligations on behalf of the Armenian people, and by the Covenant of the League of Nations, in Article 16. Whether a single state, being the neighbor of a people not organized in the fashion of western civilization, may feel justified in assuming the rôle of a tutor, a guardian, or a mandatory power without an express mandate, under Article 22 of the Covenant, is a question that, in my opinion, should be negatively answered if there were the smallest doubt about the justice of the case.

V

NATIONALITY AND MINORITIES

AFTER my last lecture, I was asked by a justly dis-
satisfied hearer if I should not, after plunging head
over heels into the troubled waters of intervention,
resume the argument of state responsibility, having
by no means exhausted it. I really intend to do so;
but I prefer to do it in my last lecture. In that lecture, I shall deal with international coöperation and
international jurisdiction, a chapter that is intimately connected with state responsibility, because
suing a state before an international court of arbitration or a court of international justice, presup-
poses a claim based on a fact that makes that state
responsible before the court. Today, I beg to con-
tinue the argument of my last lecture, on intervention, but only in so far as I wish to speak about a new
and not at all popular sort of intervention, namely,
the intervention on behalf of injured rights of minorities. The minority question affords not much
interest in happy America where immigrants of all
nations, as soon as they have set their foot on the
free American soil and breathed the American air
of liberty, begin to feel the effects of a political melt-
ing pot, in which they lose European prejudices and
gain American citizenship. Even when they remain
true to cultural traditions of their forefathers and
thereby contribute to the spiritual wealth of their
new country, they learn soon to value a free participation in a great people's sovereign power more

than an inherited allegiance to a racial minority. In
Europe, the situation is and has been quite contrary.
The minorities question is the most widespread and
most dangerous political issue of the old continent.
The Law of Nations concerning minorities is just in
the making; you will find, nevertheless, some elements of this law in Grotius. But the viewpoint of
Grotius' time was different from the modern one;
the Peace Treaty of Westfalia, 1648, regulated only
the situation of certain religious minorities, while
the conventions signed at Paris in 1919, at the same
time as the Peace Treaty of Versailles, concerned,
indeed, different sorts of minorities but kept in view,
first of all, the national minorities. In order to explain more clearly the causes of such a change in
the international public law of Europe, I shall consider first the development of the idea of a nation
and of the law of nationality, then the slow forma-
tion of international law regarding minorities, and
last the difficulties, differences, and dangers that
arise out of the nationalistic conflicts. In the sixth
lecture, I propose to deal with the means provided
by international law, since Grotius' time, for overcoming such difficulties and deciding such differences, that is to say, the means of organized international coöperation and international arbitration
or jurisdiction.

I would overstate the facts in asserting that the
idea of a national state originated in the French
Revolution of 1789; for in France (and in England
likewise) there are earlier germs of that idea. On
the other hand, I think Mr. Bernard Shaw over-
stated the facts when he made of Joan d'Arc a representative of modern nationalism. Nation, during

the Middle Ages, was more a racial than a political conception; the complicated relations now existing between nation and state were not yet in the consciousness of the peoples of Europe. The very name of that medieval Power which claimed the hegemony over Europe, the Holy Roman Empire of the German Nation, proves that the word "nation," in this connection, means something else, something less political than, for instance, the modern idea of national independence. In that Empire of the German Nation there was no general public law of a German character. While in the era of the migrations, after the fall of the antique Roman Empire, the migrating Teutonic tribes—the Goths, Francs, Alemans, Bavarians, and so on—retained their national customs, laws, and organizations even when they founded new empires throughout the vast territories of ancient Rome, and when they settled pell-mell amid the different races of subjugated peoples, the stabilized states of later Europe, during the era of feudalism and absolutism, dismissed the notion of nationality in their political and legal systems. The *libri feudorum,* the collection of statute law and case law concerning feudal institutions, are of an international character. So is the common law of Pandects, the remnant of Roman laws collected in the Institutions and Digests of Emperor Justinian, rediscovered in the time of the early Renaissance and received by the lawyers of European princes, and the law professors of European universities during the fifteenth and sixteenth centuries as a "written reason," *ratio scripta.* This reception of the Roman law did not abolish, indeed, the local laws of the different nations of Europe, but on the continent it drove them

back to mere provincialism. Statute law in the sense
of a law made by the state or the prince became binding on the subjects, whatever their nationality. The
great vassals of the old Empire possessed fiefs in
many parts of Europe, and the absolute princes of
the seventeenth and eighteenth centuries snatched
up new territories by inheritance, by war, or by
marriage wherever they had occasion to do so. The
law codes that many of those princes gave to their
peoples, for instance the *Ssvod Sakonov* of the Russian Czars, the Prussian *Landrecht* of Frederick the
Great, the Austrian Civil Code of Maria Theresa,
were not destined for a national unit but for all inhabitants of the different territories who owed allegiance to the common sovereign; even the Code Na-
poléon, bearing some marks of nationalism, is of the
same supranational character. I, for example, was
born and have lived nearly forty years under the
rules of Napoleon's excellent codification, because
my native country, the Rhineland, in the beginning
of the nineteenth century was for some years under
French dominion, and French law remained in force
there until it was superseded by the German Civil
Code in 1900. However, this disregard of public and
private law as related to national bonds ceased with
the French Revolution. The French people, fighting
for their political liberty against inner despotism
and attacked by a foreign coalition of autocrats,
found itself a nation. A few years before, the American colonies of England, fighting likewise for their
political liberty against an arbitrary government,
founded the United States of America and began to
build up a nation. The French nation, after having
driven back the invading armies of interventionist

monarchs, made of her creed concerning liberty, equality, and fraternity an article of exportation by using propaganda and armed force. You know, it is a questionable policy to apply a political principle suited to the conditions of domestic government to foreign affairs, in order to make other people go the same way in handling their own business that you found to be best for yours. Therefore, when France at the end of the nineteenth century expelled the monastic orders and tried to abolish clerical influence on education, she at the same time upheld her international claim as a protecting Power of Roman Catholic interests in the Near East. Questioned about this contradictory attitude, Gambetta answered that *L'anticléricalisme n'est pas un article d'Exportation.* However, French revolutionary ideals spread throughout Europe causing everywhere political ferment. Later on, Napoleon, the great executor of the Revolution, was compelled not only by his own indomitable energy, his military genius, and his administrative superiority, but also by the weakness of the political system then prevailing in Europe, to adopt a system of internal and external imperialism and to hold the peoples of Europe in a variegated state of political dependency. But those peoples— the Spaniards, Austrians, Russians, Prussians— with the aid of Great Britain, rose to fight their wars of liberation, hoping not only to gather for themselves the fruits of that national liberty sown by the French Revolution, but to make of them even an article of reimportation into France, just as now there are tendencies to reimport the Monroe Doctrine into the United States of America. The result of those wars of liberation was not what the people had expected; France got the Bourbons who had "learned nothing and forgotten nothing," Europe got the Holy Alliance that treated every movement of liberalism and nationalism as a felony.

Nevertheless, the nations of Europe did not forget the lesson France had taught them at the end of the eighteenth century, a lesson France itself had learned from the example of the British colonies during their War of Independence and their heroic struggle in building up the foundations of a new nation. Indeed, the United States have greatly influenced the evolution of the international law of Europe regarding the rights of a nation, as they have contributed likewise to the European concept of what a state is under international law. Those two conceptions, nation and state, developed independently and, therefore, were in danger of incessant conflict. The nineteenth century is filled with attempts of nationalism to organize all national units into independent states, and to influence the international public and private law of Europe by the ideal of identification of nation and state. The most conspicuous champions of the new political and juridical ideas were the Italian statesmen, Cavour and Mancini. Nationality began really to coincide to some extent with political organization; where national and political frontiers did not correspond, the situation was more and more considered as anomalous and needing rectification. For a modern sovereign to cede territory together with its inhabitants, like a feudal landlord who alienated his estate including the serfs, is now deemed if not against international law then certainly against political morals. This is the reason why the right of option was granted to the inhabitants of a territory ceded under a peace treaty, why it developed into the customary Law of Nations and why Napoleon III, when he struck the bargain with Cavour concerning the annexation of Nizza and Savoy, was eager to get a plebiscite from the ceded population in order to justify that bargain morally. The European practice of option and plebiscite has, you know, found a broad field of application in the peace treaties the Allies dictated to the Central Powers during the Paris Peace Conference in 1919. I hope we shall soon be able to enjoy the results of a thoroughgoing study of this matter by the publication of a work on plebiscites prepared by a prominent lady who is a member of the Williamstown Institute.

The peace treaties, in dealing with this matter, ended for the time a rapid evolution of European international law. They also bore the marks of American idealism. President Wilson, in his different declarations, became the champion of the principle called "self-determination" and he corroborated that political principle by the drastic remark that the inhabitants of a territory ought not to be shifted from one sovereignty to another like chessmen. If it really was the aim of the drafters of the peace treaties to apply in good faith this principle of self-determination, they must since then have been convinced that it has a different meaning and quite different effects in Europe and in America. In America the conception of people, nation, and state are nearly synonymous, while in Europe they are so often crossing and contradicting each other.

It is true that after the unification of the scattered parts of Italy and Germany, the nationalist movement in Europe seemed to have come to a standstill.

Nevertheless, there were left many causes of national unrest. Neither Italy nor Germany was a perfectly united nation; Italy had her Irredenta of the northern parts of the Adriatic and of the Garda Lake; Germany had severed herself from the many millions of Germans incorporated into the Austrian Duarchy. Moreover, in eastern Europe various national units experienced a growing discontent with the reigning political system. Turkey was sovereign ruler over several Christian peoples; the governing Moslem nation, the Turks, treated their infidel subjects, the Giaours, by an alternating system of disdainful indulgence of their national laws and customs and of unwarrantable brutality. The Berlin Conference of 1878 had opened for these peoples the way to self-determination, at least in Europe; but they began to go that way by fighting each other, because of conflicting national claims and aspirations. In Austria, many nations lived together rather peacefully after the Hungarian revolution was quenched in 1849 and a compromise between Austria and Hungary was reached in 1864; but the flood of nationalism rising in all Slavic parts of the Empire and backed by foreign Slavic peoples soon threatened to overflow the artificial dikes of Austria's quaint constitution. I think it is not yet sufficiently realized in this country, how much the social rising of the laboring classes in eastern Europe fostered the national movement. In becoming conscious of their natural rights the laboring classes of Austria, eastern Germany, and western Russia also became more conscious of their national claims. While in these countries the majority of the population was of Polish, Czech, or Jugoslavic origin the privileged classes were generally of German origin or they were products of German culture; for this reason, Slavic socialism and Slavic nationalism combined to struggle against the political and social system upheld in the three European empires. Today in Germany and German Austria the socialist parties are the champions of Internationalism as the best national policy, and even in Italy and in the countries of western Europe the same statement may be made with some reservations. But in the Slavic parts of Austria and Germany before the War, parliamentary representatives of the working classes would join the most ardent Pan-Slavic or nationalistic agitators. Archduke Franz Ferdinand of Austria, the presumptive successor to the imperial throne of Franz Joseph, foresaw the danger of this rising flood and planned to find an outlet by giving to the Slavic population a stronger hold on the government of the empire. If he had lived to become emperor, he most probably would have made a Triarchy out of the Duarchy; he would have constituted the Slavic peoples of the empire as an integral part of the system as Hungary was, and by these means he thought to make Austria the hegemonic power of southern Slavism. With these views he crossed not only the constitutional rights of the Hungarians but also the hegemonic ambitions of the Serbs; so he was hated by both, and he fell, a victim of Slavic nationalism and a Hermes *psychopompos*— a "leader of the slain"—of the millions of fallén heroes of the Great War. Many of you will know that fine drawing of Bonaventura Genelli, rendering the scene of Homer's Odyssey where Hermes is conducting the innumerable shadows of the dead to Hades. If the assassination of Franz Ferdinand was the immediate cause of the outbreak of the Great War, I think I am right in saying that the inadequacy of the European state system with regard to the actual distribution of European territory between the different nations of Europe has proved the most fateful fact in the whole history of that continent.

It appears from President Wilson's speeches and declarations that he was perfectly aware of this fact and tried to get that awful situation mended. But by altering the lines on the map of Europe he did not succeed in his attempt. There is no country in Europe now, excepting perhaps Portugal, where national and state frontiers are coinciding; and even in some states that seemed to be of uniform nationality before the War there appears a tendency to what the Italians call *regionalismo,* to let provincial peculiarities of today regain the force of tribal differences like those prevailing in medieval times, a tendency to decentralize the autonomy of even small national units. You may find at this time the signs of that tendency all over Europe, from the Basques and Catalans of Spain and the Macedonians of the Balkans to the Lapps of Scandinavia.

There are two countries in Europe where in spite of wide differences of nationality within the frontiers of the state the minorities problem seems to be solved effectively:—the small federal state of Switzerland and the enormous federal state of Bolshevik Russia. In my opinion, Europe will some day be called on to make a choice between those two examples of dealing with the problem of adjusting state to nation or nation to state; and, as an old liberal, I hope that she will then choose the Swiss model, not the Russian one. About the Swiss example I shall speak another time. As to the Russian pattern, I do not wish to deny that it is, in a certain direction, a standard one. Doubtful as most of the reports on Russian affairs and conditions used to be, there is no doubt about the great extent of cultural autonomy that the numerous and widely differing tribes and peoples of the Russian Union are enjoying. Local administration may be managed in the language and according to the customs of every national unit; the press is not hampered in using the national tongue by centralizing tendencies of a nationalistic bureaucracy nor does the chauvinism of a minister of education at Moscow interfere with the use of the local dialect in the school system. But there is one exception to this generous political principle of self-determination and autonomous government: To enjoy it, the people concerned must adhere to Bolshevism; they must profess the communist creed and live up to it. And you ought to bear in mind that there is no peace or armistice between the communist creed of Russian Bolshevism and any form of Christian faith. Atheism is the state religion of Russia, and whatever orders Stalin may have recently given to stop the terrorism of the godless propagandists the situation of a congregation that refuses to render to Bolshevism what they owe to God is hard indeed. During the last three or four months, I have read dozens of letters sent with great danger by members of such congregations to friends staying in Germany, and I have at the same time had opportunity to speak to Russians who have just come from there, some of whom have resolved to return to Russia in spite of the hardships awaiting them. All those records confirm the desperate position of religious minorities, if they really are minorities and not terrorized majorities. Besides the religious part of the population, the *bourgeoisie* play the rôle of a minority and a fearfully oppressed one. So in overcoming the difficulties of the national minorities problem the Bolsheviks fell into the pit of an older problem, that of confessional and feudal oppression; they seem to go back to medieval manners, but with the decisive difference that then the faithful persecuted the freethinkers, the gentry oppressed the laboring people; now in Russia freethinkers and laborers are taking their revenge. In reading Russian literature, before the War, I always had the impression of a living remnant of the Middle Ages infected with the most radical ideas of western civilization; so I did not wonder when the fearful shock of the Great War turned the Russian people topsy-turvy.

When I went to Brest-Litovsk in December, 1917, to take part in the negotiations with the Bolsheviks regarding the Armistice, and later on when I was present during the negotiations for peace with Ukraine and central Russia, I had a similar impression of a clash between two widely separated eras of human civilization. On the one side, a throng of diplomats, generals, and admirals with a grand display of uniforms, orders, ribbons, and decorations, with many people serving and waiting on them; on the other side, scarcely a dozen very clever men without any distinguishing marks on their wearing apparel, followed by a few interpreters and typewriters and guided by a lady, Madame Byzenko. She had, as a young teacher, killed the Russian Minister of War on the open street because her beloved brother, serving in the army, had been maltreated and crippled for life, and she could not get redress for his injuries. She was condemned for life to hard labor in Siberia, and twelve years afterward she was set free by the Revolution. She was bitter, harsh, and wilful, and I did not find her an agreeable conversationalist when she was my neighbor at the table of General Field Marshal Prince Leopold of Bavaria; but she was well educated; she spoke German, and when a string quartet of our German soldiers played pieces of Haydn and Schubert she sat listening to them with softened eyes, and when they had finished she rose and asked them to play Mozart also, indicating the movements of the piece she wanted on the piano that was near her. Under the layers of political and national and social hatred that separated her from the playing soldiers and from us all, there was buried, yet not dried up, the fountain of a very sensitive soul, capable of loving all that is good and true and beautiful. When Trotsky came to lead the delegation, this lady—yes, she was a murderer, but she was a lady in spite of that, this Madame Byzenko —retired to the background.

I have told you this episode just to show that there are spiritual powers capable of conquering the differences and antagonisms of national units, political systems, social classes, if we only wanted to make use of them to the proper purposes. But I do not believe that by conventions and agreements under the Law of Nations alone we are able to appease the excited chauvinism of proud peoples or the feeling of revenge that glimmers under the ashes of a lost war.

At Brest-Litovsk, we came to an agreement with the Bolsheviks about the Baltic peoples and about the German minorities in southern Russia. The Versailles Treaty has invalidated it. Combined with the other peace treaties named after Paris suburbs, it has created instead a lot of new minorities in Europe, because the Allied and Associated Powers did not apply exclusively the principle of national self-determination but also the principle of security and geographical or economical utility. Since Germany had lost the War, the application of these latter principles turned out almost entirely to her disadvantage. In many parts of Europe, the different tribes or nationalities are so mingled with one another that a clear separation by geographically warrantable lines is impossible. For such territories, the peacemakers had several possible ways to deal with the population concerned. They could treat the inhabitants, not heeding their national attachments, simply as appurtenances to the territory; but that system would have offended against the principle of self-determination and has only been applied to the Saar basin. Or they could, on the other hand, let the decision concerning the frontiers depend on a plebiscite, making the areas accessory to the majority of the people; this seemed not always advisable, because a territorial change was wanted for political reasons. Another possibility was to dispose finally of the territory and to give every individual inhabitant the right of option I have spoken of before; by this right, he could under certain conditions and within a certain time (differently fixed by the single peace treaties and for the various ceded territories) choose between the old and the new allegiance. But some of the peoples concerned did not like to have great numbers of a nationality other

than that of the governing element, the so-called
state people, having the right of option for their
state and thereby constituting an important minority.
They, therefore, tricked those would-be countrymen
with all bureaucratic skill in order to get rid of them.
Such a case was that of Bulgaria and Greece, and
that of Greece and Turkey, which led to the unhappy
proposal of Fridtjof Nansen, the great explorer and
philanthropist, to accomplish a wholesale exchange
between the minorities living on both sides of the
frontier. So in the middle of the last decade Europe
witnessed the greatest migration the history of mankind has ever known in so short a time. Millions of
people were forced to leave their homes and settle in
an unknown country not fit for their former business;
and thousands were killed by epidemics and starva-
tion. The social status of the Greek people is funda-
mentally changed by that turn of the tide bringing
colonial Greece back into old Hellas again.

Such extreme measures recalling the time of Nebu-
chadnezzar can never develop into a general rule of
international law. In most cases, the population of
the states of Europe affected or created by the Great
War remained of mixed nationality. It seemed, therefore, necessary to the principal Powers of the Paris
Peace Conference to provide for an unencumbered
political and social status of minorities, not only of
racial minorities but also of linguistic and confessional minorities. This task they carried out by the
Minority and Peace treaties made in 1919, that is to
say, the treaties concluded between the Great Powers
on one side and the newly founded or enlarged states
and the enemy states on the other side. By all the
treaties the contracting parties warranted to the

minorities of the weaker party equality of civil and political rights, unrestrained use of their language, and free profession of their faith. It would be possible to call those principles a recognized part of European international public law if the stronger parties of the minority conventions would have themselves undertaken the same obligations. But unhappily that was not the case. The one-sidedness of the treaties had two bad consequences: The minorities existing in the territories of the Great Powers and complaining of sundry offenses against their natural rights, compared their legal status with that of internationally warranted minorities and felt every injustice committed against them by their governments with double bitterness. On the other hand, the states obliged by the treaties to grant their minorities certain constitutional rights—perhaps more than they were ready to afford to anybody—those states resented the intervention of the Powers into their domestic affairs as an infringement of their sovereign rights, remarking the unwillingness of their treaty partners to assume and to fulfil the same obligations.

We may consider the Council of the League of Nations as guarantor of the minorities of Europe secured by treaty law and the Permanent Court of International Justice at The Hague as an authority of last resort. There are, however, complaints of the inefficiency of the promised guaranty because the procedure of bringing a minority complaint before the Council is very tedious and circumstantial and more fit to deter minorities from complaining than to restrain governments from discrimination. Until now the many attempts to work out a more rapid,

impartial, and efficient procedure have been wrecked
by the resistance of the states most concerned in the
matter.

Some of these states have a double interest, because they have within their frontiers minorities of
a foreign nationality and outside their frontiers
minorities of their own nationality. In such a case
you will very seldom see the government of a state
take the same attitude toward a foreigner and toward
their own minority. As an example of the situation,
not of the attitude (I am not complaining here but
explaining), I may cite Poland. Poland concluded
a treaty with the Great Powers in June, 1919, regarding foreign minorities in Poland, and it is a
signatory Power of the Versailles Treaty protecting Polish minorities in Germany. Moreover, by the
Geneva Convention of May, 1922, and some later
agreements, special regulations concerning the reciprocal minorities have been consented to.

Nevertheless, and in spite of some sentences of
general bearing that the Permanent Court of International Justice passed on German minority claims
against Poland, and a general liquidation agreement
which Germany concluded with Poland on October 31,
1929, the problem of reciprocal minorities treatment
seems not yet finally cleared. It is complicated by
other facts disturbing the neighborly relations of
the German and the Polish people, so interdependent
by economic circumstances and so closely connected
with each other by their geographical situation. Since
these facts have been mentioned by one of the lec-
turers, it is true, in a very cautious and statesmanlike manner, but, however, from a point of view

nearer to Warsaw than to Berlin, I beg to explain the German view also.

When the last Chancellor of the Empire, Prince Max of Baden, had asked for peace on the basis of the Fourteen Points of President Wilson, I counseled him, as his adviser in international law, to make in a public speech in the *Diet* certain proposals concerning the execution of the accepted principles. The speech as prepared by me was stopped by the Cabinet, who thought it would frighten our public opinion and spoil the peace negotiations. I think they were wrong—every statesman is wrong who is afraid of the truth. Now, I advised the Chancellor to propose for Poland, as the free and open access to the sea that had been demanded by President Wilson, advantages of three kinds: A free port near Danzig; the internationalization of the Vistula after the pattern of the Danube; and an internationalized railroad from Warsaw to the free port under the guaranty of the signatory Powers of the Peace Treaty. I am convinced to this day that such a regulation would have sufficed for Poland's peaceable interests. Instead, the Treaty of Versailles made the Vistula an exclusively Polish river; even those German villages that lie on the bank of the river cannot drive their cattle to water without crossing the Polish frontier. Furthermore, the Versailles Treaty gave German territory, the so-called corridor, to Poland without a plebiscite, on political grounds only, severing thereby the province of East Prussia from the rest of Germany. At last, the Versailles Treaty broke loose from the *Reich* the old German Hanse city of Danzig, calling her a free city and putting her under the protectorate of Poland as the only way of giving Poland a port on the Baltic Sea. Since then, Poland has demolished the best bridge that the Germans constructed over the Vistula, just to hinder the traffic through the corridor, and she has built up in the little fishing village of Gdingen a mighty port, using it not only as a naval base but also as a commercial center, to the detriment of the Danzig commerce. I was in Königsberg and Danzig two months ago, and I can assure you that the actual situation of these cities and the surrounding country is unendurable.

We are told the corridor must be Polish because it was under a Polish *régime* 160 years ago. In the meantime, Prussian kings have brought that territory to a flourishing state by an administration of great efficiency and integrity. Americans would be astonished indeed if Great Britain would claim the retrocession of New England on similar grounds.

We are told the corridor must be Polish because its population was of Polish origin. If it is, it was content to be a part of Germany; we never had there more of a Polish irredenta than Canada has of a French irredenta.

We are told finally that Germany must resign herself to the existence of the corridor because she may consider and treat East Prussia as a colony, outside the territory of the metropolis but easier to reach than Alaska is from Seattle or Algiers from Marseilles. I answer that you cannot compare Canada with a corridor, nor the high sea of the Mediterranean with a strip of diverted sovereignty. And as to the character of the province, it was a colony seven hundred years ago, but it is now as far from being a colony as is Pennsylvania. Twice the liberation of

German soil from foreign invasion had its origin in Prussia, and this province gave its name to a great European Power and the hegemonic state of Germany.

I will not speak about the second point of disturbance, Upper Silesia, where German and Polish claims are crashing against each other in spite of the six hundred articles of the Convention I helped to negotiate in Beuthen and Geneva in 1922. You may just as easily lay the frontier of Canada along New York's Broadway as mark the frontier to Poland between Beuthen and Kattowitz.

These facts explain the irritation of German public opinion over our eastern frontiers. I was asked recently by what means Germany could hope ever to get a better frontier in the east. I was unable to tell, for I am now not a retired minister of foreign affairs but a retired chief justice. I acknowledge that for a proud and powerful nation, especially for one that has just regained independence and sovereignty, it seems impossible to give up one bit of the fruits of an extremely clever political action resulting in national liberty, without adequate compensation. But why should statesmen despair of finding such a compensation acceptable to both parties? They ought to be patient, prudent, observant of opportunities, resolute in making use of them, and above all full of good will and ready to coöperate wherever there is an occasion.

I must sorrowfully confess that under the present circumstances I see no greater possibility of a good and durable understanding between Germany and Poland, than there was between France and Germany during the time when the question of Alsace and Lorraine was open because France could not forget that Germany had taken these provinces by a victorious war and without asking the population. But there is a difference: under the Law of Nations then in force Germany was neither forbidden to take a province as a prize of victory, nor was France hindered from waging war in order to recover what she had lost. But Germany, regarding the differences with Poland over her eastern frontiers, has thrice most formally renounced war as a means to alter them, first, by the arbitration treaty with Poland, signed in Locarno, then by her entry into the League of Nations, Article 10 of the Covenant making every member of the League a guarantor of the territorial integrity of every other member, and lastly by signing the Briand-Kellogg Pact, renouncing war altogether as a means of national policy.

When a German minister, especially a minister with military training and with a professional knowledge of the weakness of our armed force, alludes to the unsatisfactory condition of our eastern frontiers, he may have in view rather the mood of his voters than the anxieties of foreign offices and foreign newspapers; but most certainly he never dreamt of telling his people to recover the corridor by force of arms. Every member of the League may, under Article 19, prepare a demand to the Council for revision of a treaty. It seems a question of political strategy to determine how far such preparation may be made by public speeches; as a former minister of foreign affairs, I prefer the method of Gambetta: *Toujours y penser, jamais en parler.* But, after all, I never was a member of parliament, and for such a member it must be difficult not to speak about matters of importance.

Germany is in a fever, you know, the fever of electioneering. There is the probability that the radicals of both sides may win many seats because of the enormous and protracted unemployment. The less radical parties must compete with the radicals by using strong words likewise. But even if the National Socialists should, by winning an overwhelming victory, come into the embarrassing position of having to form a cabinet, they would find themselves compelled to stick to our treaties, to pay what we are owing, and to keep peace. Facts are stronger than words, and international treaties more binding than nationalist electioneering promises. Even Mr. Lloyd George, you know, could not quite get in 1919 what he had promised to his voters a year before, and he was a mighty man.

The nationalist feeling in Germany is especially roused by the extent of German minorities in Europe. No people in Europe sees such a number of its co-nationals outside of the territory of its national state, and none, perhaps the Hungarian people excepted, such a proportional number compared with the citizens of the state. I am very doubtful of minority statistics. You know, there are white lies, damned lies, and statistics, and minority statistics are of the most biased ones. But I venture to say that twelve million German people, speaking German and of German minds and customs, are living in Europe outside Germany, including Austria but excluding Switzerland. Most of them live in compact settlements, divided between twelve other states.

Many of them are, twelve years after the Armistice, suffering from political persecutions born of the war spirit or enduring hardships because of racial antagonism. So you may judge how great is Germany's interest in having the European problem of minorities solved in the spirit of humanity, charity, reciprocal recognition of natural rights, in short, of western civilization in its true and classical form.

The ghastly and terrible phantom of a war waged on behalf of subjugated minorities would disappear from the wall of old Europe's shaken political building, if every government, every governing class or nationality would bear in mind and act upon the spirit of that civilization bidding them to be fair and just to everybody, both to citizens and aliens, to co-nationals and to national foreigners. That spirit is the result not of an enthusiastic and idealistic resolution, but of a steadfast and consecutive practice of coöperation. Striving at the same noble aims of progress and of peace makes friends even of such men and such peoples as have been bitter enemies and believed it was destiny to fight each other. What is destiny? Destiny is God's will; and we are taught by Him who knows best that God's will is not hatred and war but love and peace.

VI

INTERNATIONAL COÖPERATION AND INTERNATIONAL JURISDICTION

In my last lecture I was playing a rôle that displeased many of my hearers. Indeed, I did not like it myself very much; for I am not accustomed to it. It was the rôle of an advocate. Now I have acted as a judge, as a judicial adviser of the executive, as a professor of law—but not as a barrister. On this occasion, I could not help pleading the case for my country. Since I came to the United States three weeks ago, I have often heard people say: "I am a hundred per cent American," and I liked those people. Now, you will have remarked that I am a hundred per cent German, and I hope you will not be angry with me about that. I love my country and I never knew how much I loved it until I found her vanquished, bereft of her power and wealth, mourning for her dead, and unhappy about her future. I verily believe that only those who are true to their own nation will find the way to an international understanding that has any prospect of duration, while neither busybodies who make a sport of swimming in international waters nor chauvinists who seek to exalt their own insufficient personality by brandishing the double-edged sword of national prestige, will be able to avoid most dangerous collisions. For only the true unselfish patriots, intimately acquainted with their own people's needs and desires, will be able to acknowledge similar needs and desires of

other peoples and to find rational and practical
means of giving them, as far as possible, mutual
satisfaction. They will feel, out of their own experience, the deep-rooted solidarity of mankind, especially the solidarity of sorrow—remember the universality of the unemployment scourge!—and they
will be ready to further a solidarity of happiness and
prosperity. True charity begins at home, but it does
not end at home. Christ was a true patriot, feeling
and declaring that he was first sent to the children
of Israel, his countrymen; but he did not deny his
help to aliens and he died for mankind. Therefore,
I may be easy in my mind about having chosen for
my special study international law as a law that is
binding my country sometimes against her material
interest, and I am glad, after having in my last lecture ventured into the dangerous gorges of nationalism, to return to the more promising fields of international coöperation and international jurisdiction.
Both are vehicles to and results of international
solidarity.

In nearly every one of my former lectures I have
called the attention of my audience to the fact that
the international public law of Europe, after having
since Grotius' time passed through several centuries
of growing individualism, and anarchy regarding the
relations of states to each other, begins in the twentieth century to resume the thread of medieval uni-
versalistic thought that had slipped away in consequence of the Renaissance, the Reformation, and
the reception of Roman law. The Middle Ages knew
a solidarity of the Christian nations of Europe; but
that solidarity did not have a spacious scope. Its
marks were the common creed and the common dan-

ger. A papal excommunication was of international validity; the Crusades were testimonies of an international interest in the Holy Land and the wars against Turks a joint defense of Christendom. The Turkish wars, it is true, overlap into the new era; but the later the war, the less it had a character of solidarity. Francis I of France concluded a treaty with the Sultan against the House of Hapsburg, and Frederick the Great of Prussia, more than two hundred years later, followed his example. European solidarity, never very strong in the practice, was given up even as a principle.

During all this time, there were indeed alliances and even confederations between sovereigns and vassals; but most of them were transitory expedients, not marks of a permanent unity. The only organization to which such an epithet could justly be applied was the *Hansa* or League of German towns, an association formed to protect and extend by common action, common institutions and, if necessary, by common armed force the commercial interests of all towns adhering to the League. The joint institutions of the *Hansa* were not confined to German territory, but were of an international character. For instance, the *Hansa* had settlements at Novgorod in Russia, at Wisby in Swedish Gotland, and at Trondhjem or Nidaros in Norway (a settlement called *Tyske Brygge* or German Bridge); they had a settlement on the Belgian coast called likewise Brugge, now a dead city full of remnants of its old glory; a settlement at London called the *Stahlhof* or steelyard because of the extensive importation of German hardware manufactured near Cologne; a settlement at Venice called Il Fondaco dei Tedeschi and used especially by the big commercial towns of southern Germany. These settlements resembled the modern European settlements in China and other countries of Asia and enjoyed likewise a certain amount of extraterritorial rights.

However, apart from the *Hansa* I find on the records of those times of Grotius no international association of a constructive kind. Grotius, in his chapters dealing with treaties, conventions, and agreements between kings and republics makes many distinctions between treaties public or private, personal or real, justified or unjust, durable or preliminary, authorized or unauthorized, equal or unequal, but he does not even mention the permanent associations and confederations of his time, the *Hansa* and the Swiss confederation; he devotes just a short sentence to the question of sovereignty vested in a union or a federated system of individual states, quoting Aristotle, Strabo, and Galenus, but no authority or fact of his own time. This seems to me amazing when the most important issue of his time was the dismemberment of the Holy Roman Empire and its reduction to a union of states. Indeed, that Union, the Roman Empire, and its successor, the German Confederation, though planned to realize the solidarity of the German states and to supply them with the political machinery of constructive coöperation, failed utterly in its task. Not only did the really German members of the union (competing with and distrusting each other) try by all means to frustrate a joint action, but some members of the Empire or the Confederation were members only on behalf of one part of their territory and introduced into the Union foreign interests and foreign policy. There were, for instance, Austria, Prussia, Denmark, and Sweden, and for a time even Great Britain appearing on behalf of Hanover.

You may imagine how cumbersome and difficult was the functioning of such a political machinery. When Bismarck was Prussian delegate to the German Confederation, he denounced, in official reports and private letters full of biting sarcasm, the futility of the diplomatic work of the *Bundestag*. Far worse was the situation in Grotius' time. To get a better estimate of what the machinery of the League of Nations means for Europe, I beg to tell you, following the narrative given by Sir Geoffrey Butler, the history of the negotiations that ended the terrible Thirty Years' War.

The negotiations began by an attempt at mediation made by Pope Urban VIII in 1636. The Pope sent his legate to Cologne in order to gather a conference. At his request, Imperial and Spanish representatives arrived and even Cardinal Richelieu, who in the interests of France wished to further weaken her eastern neighbors by protracting the war, seemed unable to withhold his participation. But the emperor denied passports to the Swedes, who did not then possess a legal status in the Empire but in Catholic Germany were considered as invaders or "interventionists"; and Spain refused likewise to give safe conducts to the Dutch, who had no international status at all, being rebels against the Crown of Spain. When these difficulties seemed on the point of being overcome, Lutheran Sweden, by reason of confessional anxieties, refused to come to a congress held in a Catholic city under the auspices of the Pope. Despite an attempt of the republic of Venice to get an armistice by offering her own mediation, the Congress of Cologne was an utter failure. But the Pope, in the next year, repeated his attempt; it proved to be another failure, because Sweden, as a condition of her agreeing to an armistice, demanded that somebody should pay her troops during the cessation of hostilities. Those troops lived in Germany either by French subsidies or on the country, both sources threatening to dry up during a truce. Because nobody would pay the Swedes, the second conference also broke down.

The next year, 1638, England tried without success to negotiate an agreement for a conference to be held in Brussels. At last, in 1639, Swedish and Imperial delegates in the *Hansa* city of Hamburg took the conference question into their own hands without a mediation. Their preliminary discussions led to the participation of France. However, in 1640 the discussions came to a standstill, because the French and Swedish diplomats vied with each other in raising difficulties. Problems seemed insoluble that were concerned with the form of safe-conducts, the representation on the conference of the single states of the Empire, the precedence of Sweden or France, the choice of the meeting place. Besides, the Swedes demanded from France an annual grant of one million *livres* to be paid them as long as the truce would last in order to keep their troops from plundering Germany; and France was not willing to help Germany out of the Swedish grip at so high a price. After all, a preliminary treaty was signed on Christmas, 1641, which provided for an opening of the Conference in March, 1642. The emperor was obliged to supply safe-conducts to the representatives of all

Swedish and all French allies, but between those allies there were Protestant princes of Germany whom the emperor considered as felons and to whom, therefore, he refused to supply safe-conducts. At last some statesman of that period began to formulate plans for individual, instead of general, treaty negotiations: Maximilian of Bavaria, leader of the Catholic League, with France, the Emperor with Sweden. Moreover, the question of ascertaining the full powers of delegates puzzled the cabinets extremely. No wonder that the day of opening the Conference had more than once to be postponed; instead of March, 1642, delegates assembled in the spring of 1644 and then they did not begin real business until 1645. In the meantime, innumerable questions of precedence and of full powers had to be settled; for example, the documents of the French delegates gave them authority to negotiate but not to sign and were made out in the name of the king, who was then under age, without referring to the regency.

Finally, in the summer of 1645, the first proposals for peace were brought forward by the French, in their own language, at Münster before an assembly which included twenty-six *Diet* votes, by the Swedes, in Latin, at Osnabrück before an assembly of forty *Diet* votes. Three years more of incessant negotiations were needed to formulate and to agree on the articles of the Peace Treaty of Westfalia and to lay the foundations of a new European system. Twelve years after the Conference of Cologne, diplomats and lawyers by their pettifogging allowed one of the most terrible wars Christendom has known until our own days to rage through central Europe, especially through Germany.

In the summer of 1917, Pope Benedict offered his mediation in the Great War, and the peace proposal of President Wilson failed at the end of 1916. Two years afterward, the peace treaties with the Central Powers were signed; six months and a half later, they were ratified. A long, long time for those who craved for peace; but a fairly short one compared with the experiences European peoples made with peacemaking three hundred years before. And there is another even more important difference: The Peace of Westfalia left Europe without an organization for unity; her sovereigns were free to use their independence by a foreign policy that seemed best to suit their interests, provided that if they were princes of the Empire, they fulfilled that small remainder of obligations that the treaty laid upon them. In important cases they preferred to overlook even those obligations. Therefore, on every occasion where common treaties in later times seemed advisable, the same difficulties arose as in Münster and Osnabrück. For instance, in 1698 and 1699 the negotiations that ended by the Peace of Carlowitz between Austria, the Empire, Poland, Russia, and Venice on the one side and Turkey on the other, were very complicated, and as to the Vienna Congress of 1814, it is enough to cite the joke of the Prince de Ligne: *le Congrès danse, mais il ne marche pas*. It required Napoleon's landing in Frejus and the terror that befell the diplomats to let the negotiations take a decisive step forward. However, general conferences ending in general treaties were an exception during the seventeenth and eighteenth centuries; the absence of a common treaty, which all the Powers concerned could sign, is characteristic of the diplomatic methods of that age, an age of state individualism.

If in the Europe of today a new war should break out—say a just war in the sense of the Covenant, a war allowed under Article 15—how much easier would it be, even in the case of a plurality of belligerents, to set in motion the machinery of mediation and preliminary agreement. The rules of procedure, the questions of precedence, the practice of ascertaining full powers, the immunity of delegates—all problems of this sort are, if not finally solved, at least remarkably simplified by the ten years' functioning of the League of Nations. In the Secretariat of the League, a well-informed, well-trained, internationally-minded body of men and women are kept at the disposal of mediators and of conflicting or belligerent states. The Council themselves, under Articles 12 and 13 of the Covenant, may instantly arrange a gathering of experienced statesmen in order to quench the fire of war or prevent an explosion. Rightly used, the League will spare the peoples most of that preliminary work of diplomats, official and unofficial, openly or secretly done, that in a former era took so much time and caused so much bitterness.

Certainly, the nineteenth century has done some important preparatory work. The practice of holding general political conferences has been worked out by many precedents, from the conferences of the Holy Alliance and the Pentarchy to the Paris Conference of 1856, the Berlin Conference of 1878, the Congo Conference of 1885, the Algesiras Conference of 1906, the Hague Peace Conferences of 1899 and 1907, and others. But these Conferences lacked continuity, consistency, sometimes even constructiveness. Those qualities had to be sought for in another direction.

Since the beginning of the eighteenth century, marked by the famous Methuen Treaty of 1702, the old general treaties of peace, alliance, amity, or guaranty began to give way to another form of treaty of a less political and more commercial and technical kind. Those commercial treaties mark the decline of the feudal, aristocratic era in Continental Europe and the rise of the commoners' influence, the *tiers état*, the *bourgeois* element, liberal, commercial, and industrial. The political individualism of the absolute sovereigns is reflected in the doctrine of Adam Smith. The first aim of the commercial treaties of the eighteenth and, to a great part, of the nineteenth centuries was to open as wide as possible the door of foreign countries to the free exercise of the commercial and industrial forces of the nationals of each contracting Power; the contradictory second aim, to guard domestic commerce and industry against foreign competition, is a later reaction, directed especially against Great Britain's overwhelming commercial superiority demonstrated by the economic history of Europe during many decades of the nineteenth century. Now, these commercial treaties were generally bilateral, following the individualistic trend of the era; the only link existing between them, which grew stronger as the century went on, was the most-favored-nation clauses, unreserved in European treaties, with the reservation of reciprocity or adequate concessions in the practice of the United States of America.

However, commerce and industry, starting from

individualism, soon changed the face of the world in
linking countries, peoples, and continents together,
and to such an extent that individualism soon became unable to face the problems of solidarity. As in
domestic national economy coöperative action superseded the so-called Manchester Doctrine, trade
unions, coöperative societies, and industrial associations being substituted for private enterprise and
individual labor contract, so in the sphere of international economy coöperation, common action, general agreement replaced bilateral conventions. The
first in a long series of economic or technical conventions of a universal character was the international
postal convention of 1874. To experts and interested
circles it had been long clear that the old method
of dealing by two-party treaties with international
postal service was inefficient; indeed, such treaties
kept foreign postage tariffs much higher than was
necessary, considering the national postage rates
and the real costs of delivery in the foreign country.
It was the unforgettable merit of the German Post-
master-General, Herr Stephan, that he found a way
to internationalize the postal service. After steadfast and patient preparation he convened the first
postal congress, attended by the delegates of twenty-
two states, and his efforts resulted in the foundation
of the world's postal union, probably the most universal and most durable convention existing. That
world agreement was followed by the international
telegraphic convention, the Brussels convention for
the publication of customs tariffs, the Berne conventions for the regulation of international protection of trade markets, of literary production, of submarine cables; conventions for international motor

car and air traffic, standardization of railway material, rules of seafaring, collision, rescue, and salvage. It is impossible to give an exhaustive survey of the wide range that coöperative administration of international interests won during the last fifty or sixty years; from commercial interests it spread to more spiritual, social, and moral aims, until today it includes most of the activities of European civilization.

The old treaties of peace and amity used to be either "perpetual" or without definite terms; they were often formally repealed or silently abolished when circumstances changed. The bilateral commerce treaties had generally a certain term, but with the clause of automatic prolongation, and they proved often more durable than the old "perpetual" treaties. The general or universal treaties just spoken of are distinguished from the bilateral ones by a special mark of duration: They set up international unions and founded administrative offices or bureaus charged with the application and interpretation of the articles of the convention. Many of them stipulated for the regular summons of congresses to discuss the experiences of the working of the conventional machinery; at these conferences, amendments might be proposed and easily brought to a general acceptance. The system of conventional coöperation has been the source of a new branch of international public law; "international administrative law," brilliantly expounded in the standard work of Professor Neumeyer of Munich, member of the Institute of International Law.

The foundation of the League of Nations joined the two parallel channels of modern international coöperation, the political one, characterized by general conventions of wide scope but uncertain duration, and the technical one, specialized but endowed with "stable elements"; it joined them to a great stream of perpetual international activity. While the first part of the Covenant supplies and completes all kinds of political treaties,—of individual or general treaties of peace, friendship, and arbitration,—the second part, combined with the thirteenth part of the Versailles Treaty containing the labor clauses, comprehends and collects the administrative work of all former economical and technical conventions and puts the international bureaus under the control of the League. Even those who reproach the League of Nations for having failed to fulfil its political obligations under the Covenant must concede that it has been working remarkably well in its varied administrative tasks. The League has successfully continued the practice of general technical conferences regarding problems of labor, health, traffic, and commerce; and at a large economic conference at Geneva, it tackled the complicated customs problems without instantaneous success. Disarmament in an economic sense seems to be at least as hard a nut to crack as military disarmament, because both sides of the task strike at the very heart of sovereignty—state power.

Germany was, after signing the Versailles Treaty, not favorably disposed toward the League. The relations to that body were very queer and awkward. She had been forced to sign the Covenant but was not allowed to become a member; she had all the obligations but none of the rights of membership. This mark of utter disdain shown by a society of twenty-seven nations against a people they had invited to sign a peace treaty embittered the Germans, the great majority of whom were, after the War, quite willing to take a heavy load on their shoulders in order to restore good will between themselves and their former enemies. Unhappily, that psychological moment to lay the basis of a real understanding was missed. Many resolutions and actions of the Council during the first five years of the League's existence did not add to her popularity with my countrymen. Germany's entry into the League prepared and carried out by Dr. Stresemann was consequently hailed only by a minority of our population. But I am convinced that the insight into the necessity of our joining the League, into the great advantages the League affords to her members, and into the possibilities of German coöperation especially in economic and technical matters is steadily growing in Germany. I for my part was always of the opinion that we ought to prepare for the entry and to make use of the first occasion to do so. Therefore, as early as 1920 I joined the Board of the German League of Nations Union and in 1922, after having been acquainted with the Secretariat of the League in Geneva during my negotiations with the Poles about Upper Silesia, I wrote a memorandum for Dr. Rathenau arguing that he might profit by the imminent Genoa Conference in discussing immediately with the leading statesmen of the Allies the conditions of our entry into the League. But it was too early then. France and Germany had to go before through the trial of the Ruhr invasion and of the economic breakdown, disastrous for both countries. France has since that time recovered in a wonderful way, owing to the energy, ability, and integrity of the same man who was re-

sponsible for the Ruhr struggle, M. Poincaré; while
Germany's recovery, due to the judicious policy of
Dr. Stresemann, is hampered as yet not only by the
heavy burden of her war debts but also by the world-
wide depression of trade and of every kind of production. The instability of our economic position
adds to the political tension that is shown by the turbulent scenes on occasions of electioneering propaganda in Germany. At such a time, the attention of
the politicians needs to be concentrated upon inner
affairs. After the election and the first fighting of
the parties in the new *Diet* is over I am sure the inner restlessness of Germany will quiet down. Then
she will be ready to resume her part in the great
coöperative work of the League.

To that work, a new feature is added by the Pan-
European plan of M. Briand. In my opinion, that
great French statesman has by this move shown, for
a third time after the War, his power of combining
national French interests with broad international
issues. At first he found means to collaborate with
Dr. Stresemann on French-German relations; then
he completed the disposition of the covenant regarding prevention of war by the all-embracing principle
of the Briand-Kellogg Pact; at last he tackled the
biggest of all, the restoration of the European system disjointed by the Great War and not set right by
the peace treaties. With great care M. Briand has
avoided bringing forth his plan as a revision of those
treaties; but whoever studies his memorandum at-
tentively gets the impression that something better
than the treaties is afoot. Indeed, the Versailles
Treaty—I have often declared publicly since 1919—
contains many seeds of a future law of nations leav-

ing room for a far broader international coöperation; but the seeds may only bear fruit when the one-sided and partial treaty provisions have been made reciprocal and universal. The Briand Pan-European program seems to me to be a beginning of that necessary process. The idea is closely connected with the Pan-European propaganda of the well-known Count Coudenhove-Kalergi; but M. Briand has transposed the high idealistic tunes of Count Coudenhove's propaganda to the deeper key of a realistic and essentially economic program. I think this, after the failure of the economic conference of the League, is a sufficient proof of statesmanlike courage. Consequently I am convinced that the German Government has received the message of M. Briand with deep interest and great sympathy. I know nothing of their impressions but what I have read in the newspapers; however, I believe I am right in that assumption.

Nevertheless, the European states in playing the game M. Briand bade them to be busy with should not forget that Europe is burdened with problems of even more importance than economic ones.

Eight years ago, at a meeting of the General Association of German Industries, whose general secretary I was for some time after I left office because of the signing of the Versailles Treaty, I heard Dr. Walter Rathenau, then Minister of Foreign Affairs, say emphatically: "Economy is destiny." I do not believe that. For instance, look at the dry or wet platform playing a decisive part in your next elections; that is a question involving a lot of economic consequences, but in itself it is a constitutional question; as a great British author has it, a case of "man

versus state.'' So in Europe there are many complicated differences that cannot be solved by economic
agreement. It would be unwise to suppose that European nations by tossing about the economic ball
could be made unobservant of those even more vital
issues of national liberty and national honor I have
spoken of in my fifth lecture.

Now then, how shall Europe meet the difficulties
of this vital issue? The nations have engaged not to
use armed force as a means of their national policy.
There seems to be no other means left but international arbitration or jurisdiction. But are those
measures really available in such cases? You know
that the Powers, until the Great War, declined every
form of international arbitration or jurisdiction on
questions touching their honor, their sovereignty, or
their vital interests. When, for instance, Great Britain, after the Boer War, had annexed the Transvaal
and the Orange Republics to her African dominions,
some German firms claimed payment for deliveries
they had made to the Boer Government for mining
purposes. The British Government refused to pay
them. Then the German Government took up the
claim arguing that by virtue of the international rule
of state succession a state that takes over all assets of
an annexed state has to take also its financial obligations. The British Government also refused that diplomatic claim of the *Reich*. Then our Government
proposed to settle the difference by arbitration under
the arbitration treaty concluded between Germany
and Great Britain in 1904; but the British Government replied that the case came under the so-called
clause of honor, the issue regarding vital British interests. Not agreeing with this point of view, the

German Government proposed to submit to the Court of Arbitration the previous question: Whether the rule of state succession making an annexing state responsible for obligations incurred by the annexed state would fall under the clause of vital interest. The British Government repudiating even this proposal, the German claims remained unsettled.

In the German-Swiss conciliation and arbitration treaty of 1922 it is agreed that non-justiciable differences may not be brought before the arbitration court if the defendant party makes an exception, but that, at the request of the other party, the previous question shall be decided by the court. This clause is also inserted in many other conciliation and arbitration treaties of Germany, concluded since the Great War, but not in the treaties with the United States of America, the last in a long list. The American Government preferred not to combine conciliation and arbitration in one treaty, but to make separate treaties, one of conciliation, one of arbitration, and the German Government was ready to agree to this wish.

The combination of both forms of settling a difference is a very old one. As far back as in the fifteenth century we find on record treaties between European princes or republics charging a neutral sovereign with the task of mediating or conciliating a disputed claim between them, and in the event of failure to give sentence as an arbitrator. Until the end of the nineteenth century, it was the custom of disagreeing states to give this charge only to a sovereign or a state chief, because it seemed against the prestige of an independent state to let its international disputes be settled by a private judge, a subject of another state. The old Teutonic idea that a man may only be rightly judged by his peers has left a trace in that customary Law of Nations.

This practice has been materially changed by the first Peace Conference of The Hague. The convention for peaceful settlement of international differences provided an international court of arbitration, called permanent, but consisting only of a bureau, a list of possible members to be chosen freely by the parties, and a set of rules of procedure, completed by the second Peace Conference. The advantages and the deficiencies of this system have often been explained; it has more than once done good service by avoiding European wars, especially between France and Germany (Casablanca) and between England and Russia (Doggerbank); but the great deficiency was the political bias of many sentences bearing more the character of forced compromises than of judgments under the Law of Nations. Consequently, the want of a real international jurisdiction was widely felt. The second Peace Conference at The Hague failed to provide the states with such international machinery because it was impossible to reconcile the claims of the Great Powers for a permanent influence over the Court and the claims of the minor states for an equality of membership. Europe owes to the United States the final solution of this seemingly insuperable difficulty. Mr. Root and Dr. Scott, at the Jurists' Conference of The Hague in 1920, proposed a plan for the election of members of the Permanent Court of International Justice that corresponds in an interesting manner to the famous compromise reached in the Convention at Philadelphia between the claims of the large former colonies

for permanent influence according to their importance, and the claims of the smaller states for having
their right of equal sovereignty recognized. Let us
hope that the appointments of new judges of the so-
called World Court, after the expiration of the nine-
year term, may take place without the necessity of
falling back to the measure of forming a joint committee of the Council and the Assembly.

At this late hour I do not dare to give an abstract
of the enormous and important work the Court has
done. It has made itself indispensable not only to the
members of the League, but also to the League itself.
In number and in weight, the sentences given by the
Court in a case brought before it by the disputing
states are scarcely equal to the opinions delivered
to the Council of the League, in cases submitted to
their mediatory treatment, or in points where the
Council was in doubt about how they were to manage
an administrative business of the League. The wid-
ening range of the Court's activities, the changes in
its statute and its rules, and above all the adherence
of so many states to the optional clause of the Court
protocol are things so well known that I must for-
bear to dwell on them. It was history, not current
policy, that I proposed and promised to speak about
before the Institute of Politics at Williamstown.
However, in concluding my last lecture and my
course I may be allowed to look a bit into the future.
I have explained the development of international
coöperation and of international jurisdiction in Europe. The acme of international coöperation I found
in the League of Nations, the acme of international
jurisdiction in the World Court. But the League of
Nations is only a league of some nations as long as

the United States is not a member; and the World
Court is only a court of local jurisdiction as long
as the United States of America is not a member.
Therefore, I conclude my lectures by crossing the
Atlantic and asking: What will the United States of
America do? I hear very different answers. Generally speaking, there seems to me to be more votes
in favor of joining the Court than in favor of joining
the League. I am far from giving my own opinion in
a case that only Americans have to decide; but it may
be of interest to hear from a German what in this
connection would be the preponderant feeling in his
country. I am sure the news that America had entered the League would be accepted as tidings of
great joy, because no European Power would, in
European differences, enjoy such credit for impartiality in cases of council mediation as the United
States. As to the Court, the joy would be greater
still. I myself lay even more stress on America's
joining the Court than on joining the League. For
there is a danger of a split in the Law of Nations, a
split between a European and an American international law. Such a split would be of most fatal consequences. If afterward a difference between an
American and a European state should arise, under
which law would the court of arbitration or of justice find the verdict? To have one sole court is the
condition of having unity of law; the Supreme Court
at Washington is the best proof of this truth. No
codification of internal law will hinder the disinte-
gration of that law, when its interpretation and application is left to different tribunals of last resort.

Nevertheless, the adherence of the United States
to the protocol of the Hague Court might be fatal to

its functions when the consequence would be to over-
burden the Court with international lawsuits. Today
already the business of the Court is very large. The
European Powers, to make room for the entry of new
members of the Court association, ought to be very
reluctant to bring their differences before that au-
gust body without strict necessity. To have renounced
war as a means of national policy does not mean
bringing all quarrels before the Court. In private life
and in the life of states the best member of the society and the most agreeable is not he who renounces
force by suing his neighbor before the court, but he
who even renounces a lawsuit in order to make friends
with his neighbor. And the best statesman, in my
opinion, is the man who needs neither generals nor
admirals nor judges nor arbitrators to secure, in a
difference with another state, the interests of his
country.

ERRATA

Page 144, line 13, first column : for Macoby read Maccoby

Page 146, line 23, first column : for *Regnum* read *Regum*

INDEX

Peace, laws of, 23–24; maintenance of, 40
Peloponnesian War, 51
Pentarchy, the, 89, 127
Permanent Court of Arbitration, 94, 136, 137
Permanent Court of International Justice, 66, 67, 111
Persian War, 51
Plebiscite, 102, 109
Poincaré, 133
Poland, 27, 28, 115–116; and foreign minorities, 112
Pope, the, and Peace of Westfalia, 16; and mediation, 123, 126
Portugal, 105
Postal service, internationalization of, 129
Privateering, 30, 33–37; and naval service, 35; outlawed, 36
Prize Courts, American, 62; British, 32, 58
''Productive Pledges,'' 92
Protocol of Geneva, 63
Prussia, 32; East, 114
Puerto Cabello, 94

Rathenau, Dr. Walter, 132; quoted, 134
Reciprocity, 128
Reclamations, doctrine of, 81
Red Cross, International, 44, 45
Reformation, the, 11, 12
Regionalismo, 105
Reparations, 93
Reprisals, 29–33, 84; abolition of, 31; international, 30; law of, 31–32; private, 30, 80
Richelieu, Cardinal, 13, 123
Root, Elihu, 79, 137
Rousseau, 18; his theory of social contract, 18
Ruhr District, invasion of, 92, 132–133
Russia, and the Versailles Treaty, 69

Russo-Japanese War of 1904, 87

Saguntum, 29
San Stefano, Treaty of, 85
Schill, 26
Schuecking, Prof., 67
Scott, Dr., 137
Self-determination, 102, 103, 109
Seven Years' War, 35, 36
Shaw, George Bernard, 97
Shimonoseki, Treaty of, 87, 88
Siéyès, Abbé de, 9
Silesia, 115
Smith, Adam, 128
Socialism, 3, 104
Socialists, National, 117
Société Suisse de Surveillance Économique, 59
Sovereignty, 10, 12–14, 17–18, 31, 71, 122, 131; absolute, 128; division of, 75; equal, 138; and just war, 45; limits of, 74; national, 20–22; split, 83, 84
Soviet Government, and international obligations, 84
Spitzberg Islands, 65
Ssvod Sakonov, 99
Stalin, 106
State, the, and disarmament, 41; European system of, 105; evolution of, 7–9; federated, 122; feudal, 8; and foreign liabilities, 78, 79, 82, 84; guardianship, 74; individualism of, 127; medieval, 6; modern, 6, 7, 10, 23; national, 97; personality of, 10, 23; power of, 18, 21; responsibility of, 30, 71, 74, 77, 78, 81, 83, 84, 94; socialism, 74; sovereignty of, 6, 22, 23, 71, 111, 131; succession of, 135, 136; system of, 18
Stephan, 129
Strabo, 122
Stresemann, Dr., 132, 133
Suez Canal, 65, 68
Swiss Confederation, 122